"Written in clear, persuasive and effective style, Russell Gough's *Character Is Everything: Promoting Ethical Excellence in Sports* shares with us a message we all need to rehear: Sports ought to be a character-building activity, not merely a cash machine."

**– Amitai Etzioni, Professor, George Washington University
and author of *The Spirit of Community***

"I believe that Russell Gough provides a different approach to ethics and character in sport that is appropriate for increased public understanding about fair play in sport. This book provides useful insight to the sport and ethics arena and I would recommend it to all individuals who are interested in making sport a positive experience."

**– Judith C. Young, Executive Director of the National
Association for Sport & Physical Education**

"I am pleased to recognize the efforts of Russell Gough's *Character Is Everything* as a means to promote the true essence of sport. The conscious awareness of the impact we, who are involved in these activities, can have on others through this medium cannot be overemphasized as we fulfill our responsibilities. I congratulate Dr. Gough for his initiative in providing this reminder to us."

**– Robert F. Kanaby, Executive Director of the National
Federation of State High School Associations**

"*Character Is Everything* is unquestionably the most thought provoking and best developed of the books on sportsmanship and ethics that the Institute has reviewed. It covers the important points, and the language is clear enough to cause people to think and to engage in dialogue. Perhaps most importantly, it is a book that will clearly appeal to both coaches and parents—the two most important targets in the implementation of sportsmanship-like practices."

**– Dan Doyle, Executive Director of the Institute for
International Sport**

D0075118

"Primordial principles are redefined by each new generation; this is an excellent handbook to guide ours. *Character Is Everything: Promoting Ethical Excellence in Sports* challenges us to think about personal attitudes and behavior both inside and outside the sport arena."

> – **Joan Price, Manager of the Drug Testing Program, United States Olympic Committee**

"This book addresses not only the central problem of sports in our society, but that of our culture generally—the erosion of moral and ethical standards. It emphasizes the importance of the role of each of us in promoting respect for fundamental values and ethical behavior that result in development of good character that causes one to consistently do the right thing."

> – **Wilford S. Bailey, President Emeritus of Auburn University and Past President of the National Collegiate Athletic Association**

"Gough has used a very creative and effective way to approach the subject of sportsmanship. This book will hold your attention from start to finish. I highly recommend it to anyone concerned about the future of amateur athletics."

> – **Karen Hellyer, Assistant Commissioner of the California Interscholastic Federation–Southern Section**

"Coaches and players at all levels, as well as people who participate in sports solely for recreation, can benefit from reading this book. The emphasis on character and character building being a key to displaying sportsmanship and ethics in sport is a terrific and significant point. It clearly marks a path for those wishing to demonstrate ethical conduct in sports."

> – **Jim Haney, Executive Director of the National Association of Basketball Coaches**

"*Character Is Everything* should be read by every individual who is involved in or cares about intercollegiate athletics. All of us need to take its message very seriously."

> – **George Raveling, former head basketball coach, University of Southern California; television analyst**

Character Is Everything
Promoting Ethical Excellence in Sports

Character Is Everything
Promoting Ethical Excellence in Sports

Russell W. Gough
Pepperdine University

DISCARD

Harcourt Brace College Publishers

Fort Worth Philadelphia San Diego New York Orlando Austin San Antonio
Toronto Montreal London Sydney Tokyo

Publisher	Christopher P. Klein
Senior Acquisitions Editor	David C. Tatom
Developmental Editor	Marnie Oldham
Project Editor	Tamara Neff Vardy
Production Manager	Diane Gray
Art Director	Candice Clifford
Cover Illustration	Mary Thelen

Requests for permission to make copies of any part of the work should be mailed to: Permissions Department, Harcourt Brace & Company, 6277 Sea Harbor Drive, Orlando, Florida 32887-6777.

Address for editorial correspondence to: Harcourt Brace College Publishers, 301 Commerce Street, Suite 3700, Fort Worth, TX 76102.

Address orders to: Harcourt Brace & Company, 6277 Sea Harbor Drive, Orlando, FL 32877-6777. 1-800-782-4479 or 1-800-433-0001 (in Florida).

ISBN: 0-15-503528-2

Library of Congress Catalog Card Number: 96-075980

Printed in the United States of America

6 7 8 9 0 1 2 3 4 5   016   9 8 7 6 5 4 3 2 1

For individual orders call 1-800-831-7799.

To Mr. Tae Wae Haw

Acknowledgments

I would like to express my appreciation to Pepperdine University, in particular to Dwayne VanRheenen, dean of the faculty, and David Baird, chair of the humanities division, for release time to complete the writing of this book and for their commitment to the paramount importance of character education.

I am extremely grateful to the following reviewers commissioned by Harcourt Brace: Dan Doyle, John Gerdy, Jim Haney, Scott Kretchmar, Jim O'Brien, Joan Price, John Secia, and Rich Seils. For their constructive and invaluable feedback—and especially for their unanimous support of the purpose of and need for *Character Is Everything*—I offer a very sincere thank-you.

One of these readers deserves a very special word of appreciation: John Secia, for his painstaking editorial assistance on the original manuscript, his timely and much-needed pep talks, and his I'm-always-there-for-you spirit. From beginning to end, *Character Is Everything* has been significantly improved because of the personal sacrifices John made in time and energy, and I am greatly in his debt.

For their very helpful and conscientious "reviews" of the book, I'd like to express my thanks to each of my fall 1995 sports ethics seminar students: Kevin Ahaesy, Tezale Archie, Tarik Bragg, Cathy Carone, Justin Cuellar, Quentin Gebeau, Eric Griffin, J. T. Harrison, Lance Jordan, Irene Mababa, Jennifer Newman, Maggie O'Connell, Robert Presley, Nicole Price, Debbie Prouse, Amanda Spoor, Matt Stewart, Niki Tuminaro, Anne Vicker, Matthew Williams, and Jim Yates.

It was both a professional and personal pleasure to work with the Harcourt Brace staff, in particular with Bill Brisick, Steve Drummond, Marnie Oldham, David Tatom, Tamara Vardy, Diane Gray, Candice Clifford, and Kim Standish. For their unfailing courtesy, professionalism, and expertise, I am truly grateful.

Among the many other friends, colleagues, and family members to whom, in both tangible and intangible ways, I am indebted, I would like to express heartfelt thanks to Jeff Bliss, Gary Brown, Donovan Gay, Ron Jeziorski, Roberta Ostrander, Rubel Shelly, Jeff Tuckness, and Dave Worth.

Above all, I want to express my deepest appreciation to Jeannine Gough—my wife, best friend, and role model par excellence. I simply can't thank her enough for always being the first to read and give feedback on each new section of the manuscript, and for almost single-handedly caring for our home and, especially, for our young son, Nicholas, while I was writing the manuscript—and all of *this* while she was expecting our second child, Gabriella. Without her extraordinary patience and support, *Character Is Everything* certainly wouldn't have been written as quickly, and might not have been written at all.

Sports are wonderful; they can bring you comfort and pleasure for the rest of your life. Sports can teach you so much about yourself, your emotions and character, how to be resolute in moments of crisis and how to fight back from the brink of defeat. In this respect, the lessons of sports cannot be duplicated easily; you quickly discover your limits but you can also build self-confidence and a positive sense of yourself. Never think of yourself as being above sports.

– Arthur Ashe (in *Days of Grace*, written shortly before his death in 1993)

Contents

Role Models:
   Getting Clear on the Concept   55

Ethical Excellence:
   The Name of the Game Js Always
   My Personal Character   71

Extra Points:
   Taking Jt to the Next Level   91

Starting Points:
Caring About the Game

The ball's in our court.
Your court and my court. Our court. It will never be in anyone
    else's court.
And that's precisely what this book is all about.

Three factors—one positive, one neutral, one negative—have
compelled me to write *Character Is Everything*. First, I couldn't
agree more with Arthur Ashe's eloquent words in the epigraph.
Sports can teach. Sports can shape. Sports can unify. Sports can
comfort. Sports can uplift. Sports can indeed do many positive
things—not always, and not always perfectly, but they *can*.
That's the important point.

In the spirit of Ashe's words of wisdom, it is my hope that this
book can help breathe some new life into that old and much-used
adage "sport builds character"—an adage many people in and out
of the sports arena have, unfortunately yet understandably, come to
see as passé at best or false at worst. But, of course, there are far
more athletes, coaches, parents, physical educators, school administrators, community leaders, sportswriters, social scientists, and
even ethics educators who view "sport builds character" as far from
passé or false. There is indeed plenty of evidence to suggest that, in
many instances, sports continue to shape character in positive, life-
enriching ways.

While debates continue about whether sports are in fact having a positive influence on personal character, or even societal
character, I have written *Character Is Everything* simply on the
premise that sports *can* have such a positive influence. This
premise is crucial: If our belief in the potential for good dies—in
other words, if our belief that "sport builds character" dies—
our sports culture will likely die with it.

Second, for better or worse, our society is madly in love with sports competition. When you consider that, by some estimates, more than 96 percent of the American people play, watch, or read about sports with some frequency, that 70 percent follow sports every single day of the week, that 42 percent actually participate in a sport daily, and that more than 25 million young adults and children participate in at least one organized sport each year, you begin to see why many scholars think sports are second only to religion in this country in cultural scope and significance. For a majority of Americans, sports have clearly become a highly valued part of our way of life.

Whether this all-pervasive passion for sports competition is ultimately good or bad for society is—and will continue to be—an open question. But what is not an open question is whether this passion has the *potential* to do a great deal of good or bad. It clearly does, and that's why we cannot take for granted how profoundly sports competition can shape an individual's, as well as society's, beliefs, attitudes, and actions.

Third, especially because sports have become such a powerful cultural force, there is an urgent need to take much more seriously the *ethical* dimension of our games. Have you ever taken the time to think about what "ethics" means and how ethics relates to sports? What about the relationship between ethics and sportsmanship? Encouragingly, many schools and athletic organizations across the country are already giving pointed attention to these questions. But each one of us who truly cares about what is happening to our games must do so as well.

Why? Our sports culture, like our society in general, is clearly suffering from an erosion of ethical values, attitudes, and conduct. None of us likes to dwell on this negative reality, but it *is* a reality. Although a great many sporting events continue to be characterized by sportsmanship and fair play, it's increasingly difficult to deny that our nation's sports, both professional and amateur, are showing disturbing signs of ethical erosion. On this particular point, even the most casual sports fan needs no statistics.

Drug abuse, cheating, gambling, distrust, greed, egotism, racism, sexism, violence. Trash talking, showboating, temper tantrums, bench-clearing brawls, disrespect for opponents and for game officials, and grossly unrealistic pressures and expectations. You name it, the categories on the sports dishonor roll seem to keep growing both in number and intensity. Think about it: When was the last week you *didn't* read or hear about some on-the-court or off-the-court unsportsmanlike incident?

It's no doubt difficult, if not impossible, to quantify precisely just how much this ethical erosion has affected sports and those of us involved with them. But we would be fooling ourselves if we didn't at least conclude that our sports culture seems to be succumbing more and more to "winning is everything," and "win at all costs" attitudes. Despite the old and wise saying, "It's just a game," many of our games are no longer *just* games. They've become ethical minefields, characterized by obscenely high stakes and warped do-or-die values. And let's not be lulled into thinking that this is only true of professional sports. Unfortunately, it's true all the way from Little League to the big leagues.

When you combine the three things just described—sports' potential for good, sports competition's pervasiveness in the American way of life, and the erosion of ethical values within sports—you begin to get a good idea why this kind of book is needed and why its subject can go well beyond sports to the heart of society itself. At the very least, no matter what level of sports we're involved with and no matter how we're involved—as athlete, coach, parent, educator, official, executive, athletic booster, or casual fan—we all should be concerned.

Indeed, we *must* be concerned. And we must do all we can to move beyond merely "talking the talk" about sportsmanship and the essential need for ethical values in sports. Make no mistake about it: Our sports and our society depend on these values.

If there ever has been a time to do all we can to promote these values and stem the tide of unsportsmanlike attitudes and conduct, it is now.

This book represents one small effort to do what needs to be done.

There's no time like the present.

To have a better idea of what I am attempting to say and do in this book, it will help for you to know three things about my approach:

First, *this book tries to strike a balance between the positive and negative, and between the idealistic and realistic.* If, overall, it leans toward one side more than the other, I certainly hope it's the positive side. We get more than enough negativity and cynicism about sports these days: about how sports no longer build character, how some coach is a bad role model, how yet another athlete has been arrested and charged with some crime. Many of the reports we hear are true, some are overblown, others are just false. And it's not my intention here to single out the media, even if the media do at times overemphasize the negative and the cynical because those sell so well.

We must remember that negativity and cynicism represent a two-way street: They sell, but they also *buy.*

The point is that we need to keep our negativity and cynicism in perspective and in check. Based on my own experience, I'm convinced that efforts to promote ethical excellence and sportsmanship are most successful when done in positive and proactive ways. Being negative in our approach, by emphasizing primarily or only what is wrong, won't take us very far down the road of ethical excellence.

In fact, if we let them go too far, our negativity and cynicism will prevent us from taking that road at all. Negative approaches never give anyone a strong and lasting incentive for doing what is right and good. Only a strong and lasting emphasis on what is right and good can give someone a strong and lasting incentive for *doing* what is right and good.

Second, unlike many books treating ethical issues in recent years, *this book focuses primarily on basic ethical issues in sports that are largely, if not completely, noncontroversial.* For two reasons, I have not attempted to tackle highly controversial and complicated ethical "dilemmas" that can arise in sports:

- While there is no doubt we are confronted at times with controversial and complicated ethical dilemmas in our lives, they are very much the exception, not the rule. My intent is not in the least to minimize their importance, but to highlight the fact that on a day to day, game to

game basis we usually have a clear idea of the line sepa-
rating the right thing to do from the wrong thing to do.

- These ethical dilemmas have been emphasized and
exploited so much that many people have gotten the
impression that ethics is nothing but personal opinion
and debate about dilemmas and that to talk about
ethics always results in endless controversy. This is a
very wrong and dangerous impression. In part, this
book has been written as a reminder that, in some of
the most important and fundamental ways, ethics is
anything but controversial and complicated.

Third, partly in the spirit of its positive and proactive approach,
this is a "mirroring," rather than a "finger-pointing" book. In a
conversational, one-on-one style, I'm asking that each of us think
about these basic issues in terms of our own individual attitudes and
behavior, *not* in terms of someone else's attitudes and behavior. The
decision to write the book this way was largely motivated by my
concern that many of us have become all too accustomed to pointing a finger and finding fault in others—in *their* fans, in *his* team,
in *her* coach, in *my* teammates, or in *that* sportswriter—without
taking the time to look in the proverbial mirror.

What about *my* attitude and *my* actions?

Many of us have had a minister, priest, or rabbi remind us time
and time again that, before we are too quick to point out the tooth-
pick-sized fault in someone else's eye, we should stop and consider
whether we have a telephone pole–sized fault in our own. Toward
the goal of helping to foster that wise and time-honored attitude,
this book never names names (unless in a positive light), never
assassinates anyone's character (an unfortunately popular sport
these days), and never suggests how things would be better if only
he or *she* or *they* would get their act together (which is always easy
to say but is not very helpful).

Finally, while relatively short, *this book takes an approach
that can go a long way toward resolving many, if not most, of the
ethical problems that increasingly plague sports and society in general.* This approach, as you'll see, is simple yet difficult, idealistic
yet practical, inexpensive yet costly, and distant yet close to home.

It's also important to state at the beginning that the substance of this approach is not my creation. While I can assume responsibility for not describing it as fully or clearly as it might have been described, I can take no credit for its truth and wisdom. It's an approach that has been cultivated throughout human history by many different groups of people. It's an approach that transcends virtually all political, ethnic, and religious boundaries and that has perhaps proved as successful as any approach can in promoting ethical excellence.

Most important of all, this approach provides solutions that are not found in *this* governing body or *that* rule book, *this* athlete or *that* official, *his* parents or *her* friends, *your* fans or *your* coaches, but are found in *my* own character. The answer begins and ends with individual character.

Character *is* everything.

Character Is Everything
Promoting Ethical Excellence in Sports

Sportsmanship:

A Reality Check

Avoiding Extremes

Sportsmanship is dead.
Sport no longer builds character.
Athletes are not good role models.
"Sports ethics" is a contradiction in terms.
These days sports and sportsmanship
are nothing but oil and water.

You've probably heard your share of remarks like these, especially if you're an athlete or a coach.

If I had a nickel for every time I've heard one of them, I'd be buying Lakers or Dodgers season tickets. As someone who spends much of his time teaching, speaking, and writing about ethics, I've learned that sweeping, cynical remarks like these come with the territory. Whenever I teach courses or write articles about "business ethics," or "medical ethics," or "political ethics," I get the same types and numbers of remarks. Sometimes they're made with tongue in cheek, sometimes not. But they're definitely made often these days.

The problem is that, while remarks like these are understandable, they aren't very helpful. They blur our perspective more than sharpen it. And they can come back to haunt us. Big time.

Notice how these kinds of remarks tend to put things in such extreme either-or terms, as if there were no middle ground. As if "sportsmanship" and "sports," "sports" and "ethics," "sports" and "character building," "athletes" and "good role models" were polar opposites. As if an athlete were completely a good role model or not one at all. As if sports always built character or never did. As if our games were completely sportsmanlike or completely unsportsmanlike.

However, the fact of the matter is this. That middle ground is usually very large, and it's where we almost always find ourselves: somewhere between being completely sportsmanlike and being completely unsportsmanlike, somewhere between being a perfect role model and being a terrible role model.

One of the greatest dangers of this cynical either-or mentality is the way it can eventually force us into seeing only the bad and not the good that still exists in our games, in our athletes and coaches, in ourselves.

But it goes even deeper than that. Notice also how sweeping either-or remarks like "athletes are not good role models" are not just remarks. They're *judgments*. Sweeping judgments. And as sweeping judgments, they're not just unhelpful. More often than not they're unfair, unbalanced, and untrue as well.

The crucial point here is that making these kinds of judgments is serious business. And if there's any doubt as to how serious it is, all we have to do is consider how it can come back to haunt us. It's easy for us to see that judgments like "athletes are not good role models" can be pretty serious because they are far too general and are unfair, but how would we like it if someone said that *we* were not good role models? Or that our team was a bunch of cheaters? That's easy enough to answer: We'd say that we were being judged, that we didn't like it, that it was unfair.

But more importantly, let's try turning the tables: How would other people feel when you or I said that *they* weren't good role models? Or that their team was a bunch of cheaters? They would no doubt say that we were also judging them, that they didn't like it, that it was unfair. And, of course, they would be right. There's just no way around it.

Please don't misunderstand. The point isn't that we should *never* make judgments. That would be bad advice that's highly unrealistic.

Sometimes we simply have to make judgments and act on them. If some of our teammates are regularly using drugs after practice hours, our judgment that they are wrong in using drugs *and* that we should not hang around them outside practice is a wise and justified judgment. If the player who is guarding you during a game commits a flagrant foul by deliberately throwing an elbow at your head, you are undoubtedly justified in saying that he or she was wrong or unsportsmanlike in that action.

But it's one thing to say that a certain athlete was wrong or unsportsmanlike for taking a cheap shot, and it's quite another thing to make a blanket statement that he or she is not a role model. In one instance, we are primarily making a judgment about an *action;* in the other, we are making a sweeping judgment about the whole *person.* (As I'll mention later in discussing role models, most of us are seldom in a position to make such sweeping judgments about other players and coaches.)

The point is simply that judging other people, especially judging their character in a sweeping either-or way, is serious and risky business. For example, what if we read in the paper that an athlete or a coach has been suspended for unsportsmanlike conduct, and we are quick to conclude that "he has no character" or "she's not a role model?" Why would we be so quick to conclude this? Not a single one of us wants to be judged in this way. We all make mistakes at times. Sometimes we lose our cool; sometimes we treat an official disrespectfully; sometimes we bend the rules; sometimes we even break the rules. But each one of us hopes that no one will judge us based simply on our mistakes, that everyone else will see we are still basically good despite our mistakes.

That's the reality. None of us wants to be at the receiving end of sweeping either-or judgments. They're definitely unfair, but let's face it: More than anything else, they hurt.

---

66 One player practicing sportsmanship is far better than fifty preaching it. 99

Knute Rockne

If Unsportsmanlike Conduct Was Like Air Pollution

What we need to do is to find more balanced and realistic ways to talk about sportsmanship and ethics without resorting to extremes.

One way that I have found very helpful to talk about these important issues is in terms of *air quality*. So, for example, we could talk about unsportsmanlike attitudes and conduct in terms of pollution. This approach for talking about sportsmanship and ethics occurred to me during an intense, one-on-one discussion that I once had with the coach of a high-profile, pressure-cooker college basketball program. A well-respected and successful coach, he remarked to me that unsportsmanlike attitudes on and especially off the court were making it more and more difficult for honest coaches and student athletes "to breathe freely and easily while trying to do the right thing."

"My wife tells me I need some fresh air," he said in a dejected tone of voice. "The game is much, much more than a game now... Too much bad air. . . . Makes you wanna choke sometimes."

Difficult to breathe freely and easily.
Need some fresh air.
Too much bad air.
Makes you wanna choke sometimes.

Struck by his candid comments, I started asking myself several questions like this one: If unsportsmanlike attitudes and conduct are in fact like air pollution, to what extent would we say that our sports world has become dangerous to our health?

This analogy is useful because it allows us to talk in terms of degrees, rather than in either-or extremes. As everyone knows, southern California (where I live) is known for its smog. But notice how it would be wrong to conclude that the air in southern California is unhealthy, just as it would be wrong to conclude that sportsmanship is dead in America. Sweeping generalizations like these aren't helpful, especially because they're so misleading.

In fact, many places in southern California have very clean air, some have moderately clean air, and a few—especially in the Los Angeles basin—indeed have very unclean air at times. (But for much of the year, the air in the Los Angeles basin is anything but unhealthy!) Air quality in southern California depends, of course, on several things: general location (valley, coast, mountains, or desert), exact location (the part of the valley, the part of the coast), weather (hot or cold, windy or calm, sun or clouds), and time of year, among others.

The same is true about the "air quality" of our sports world. It's simply unfair—not to mention untrue—when someone says that sportsmanship is dead in our country, as if all our sports events were being played in "first stage alert" atmospheric conditions. (In Los Angeles, weather forecasters announce a "first stage alert" on days when the smog is so unhealthy that people are encouraged to stay indoors.)

Like the quality of the air we actually breathe, the air quality in our particular corner of the sports world will depend on various factors, such as these:

- the type of sport (baseball? soccer? hockey? swimming? lacrosse? mountain climbing?)
- the level of competition (Little League? interscholastic? backyard? intercollegiate? professional?)
- the rules of a given sport (Do they encourage sportsmanship? Are there enough rules? Are there too many needless rules? Do the rules promote trust among competitors?)

- the kinds of pressures involved (competitive? peer? psychological? family?)
- the kinds of rewards involved (financial? educational? psychological? physical?)

and, most importantly:

- the characters and attitudes of the people involved (players, coaches, game officials, league officials, fans, and so forth)

There are other factors that could be listed. But given just these six important factors, how would you go about answering the question asked earlier: *If unsportsmanlike attitudes and conduct are in fact like air pollution, to what extent would we say that our sports world has become dangerous to our health?*

You're probably expecting me to offer an answer here. But I'm not going to, and that's not a cop-out. Because aside from saying what is obvious—that our sports world in general is suffering from unsportsmanlike pollution—I really *can't* answer it for you. It's very important that I'm asking *you* this question, because no one else can presume to answer it for you. There are just too many intangibles involved. It's not as though we could simply go to the sports pages, find an "unsportsmanlike pollution index," and determine just how bad the air was on a given game day in someone's particular corner of the sports world. Obviously, we can't measure unsportsmanlike pollution half as precisely as we can measure air pollution.

So unless I or someone else were to take the time to really get to know your game, your league, your coaches, and your players, I couldn't—shouldn't—try to make a judgment.

But *you* can. And *you* should.

I'll be the first to agree if you say that you don't like people "should-ing" at you, that when people "should" at you, you feel like "should-ing" back to them. But there are some "shoulds" we can't avoid, or can't afford to avoid. And this is one of them—*if* we do in fact care about the health and future of our games.

❝ The greatest opportunities for sportsmanlike conduct arise where there are the greatest opportunities for unsportsmanlike conduct.❞

R. G.

That's the most important point of this chapter. *You* should try to make an honest assessment of the air quality in *your* specific corner of the sports world, just as *I* should in *mine*. This kind of business is not only serious, it's necessary.

The health of our sports, as well as *your* health and *my* health, depend on it. That's the reality.

One final note from the for-what-it's-worth column.

If my numerous visits to and associations with high schools, colleges, and national sports organizations have taught me any-thing, it is this: Don't be too surprised if you're surprised by what you find when you make an honest effort to assess unsportsmanlike pollution. Things are not always as they appear, no matter what the level of competition. Despite what we have read or heard, the air may not be so polluted. Conversely, what may seem like healthy air may in reality not be so healthy at all.

The #1 Pollutant:
The "No Place for Second Place" Attitude

While it may be difficult to determine just how much pollution is in our sports atmosphere, we can easily determine what is polluting the game more than anything else.

Whenever I think about this #1 pollutant, as well as about what's needed to clean it up, I can't help but think about the 1994 Winter Olympics in Lillehammer, Norway. Like many of our sporting events, those Games were a study in contrasts: Some very good air mixed with some very bad air.

On one hand, there was the applause—awesome, thunderous approval from countless Norwegian fans applauding every Norwegian athlete as though he or she had won first place. If the athlete won second place, third place, or came in last place, it didn't matter. Thunderous applause ensued every time. All places were *first* places. Every Norwegian competitor was a winner.

It was as if each and every round of applause generated a resounding blast of fresh perspective: Losing did not make one a loser. Winning was emphatically *not* everything.

The Norwegian fans' message was loud and clear: No matter how you performed, you were accepted. Valued. Legitimized.

There was a place for second place. Even a place for last place.

On the other hand, of course, there was that vicious attack on ice-skater Nancy Kerrigan. That attack demonstrated how competing for the gold had evolved into a literal and violent gold rush. That attack symbolized the extent to which certain forces in our sports world are attempting to completely illegitimize second place. That attack forever remains a disturbing symbol of our sports world's #1 pollutant: The "no place for second place" attitude.

This attitude pollutes our games by devaluing second place. Not to mention third place, last place—any place but first. Second place becomes no place, a valueless wasteland for losers. If you aren't #1, you aren't worth much, if anything.

What I'm describing as the "no place for second place" attitude, of course, is essentially the same thing as what we've always called the "winning is everything" attitude. But in certain respects "no place for second place" gets to the heart of the matter more directly, because it reminds us of exactly what is so bad about this mentality: It's not simply that winning is given too much value, it's that everything else is essentially given *no* value. And "everything else" involves people, all of whom have tremendous value whether they ever step on a court or field of play or not.

It's difficult to exaggerate the importance of this last point, because what is ultimately being devalued by the "no place for second place" attitude is not where one places, but *people* themselves. Individual people with names and faces, with families, with friends, with aspirations, with feelings, and with strengths and weaknesses just like you and me.

Sometimes it's all to easy to see this destructive pollutant at work.

Some instances of the "no place for second place" attitude are easy to recognize because they are so extreme, as when we heard about the much-publicized attack on Kerrigan. Or when we hear that Olympic athletes have been disqualified for using

---

❝Character is always lost when a high ideal is sacrificed on the altar of conformity and popularity.❞

Anonymous

steroids. Or that a college athletic program has been given the "death penalty" by the National Collegiate Athletic Association for major rules violations. Or that a high school coach has been fired for hitting a player. Or that college-bound athletes have been ruled ineligible to participate for cheating on their entrance exams. Or that two professional athletes have been fined and suspended for a bloody brawl. You get the picture.

But many other instances of the "no place for second place" attitude are more subtle. They may not be so easy to recognize at first. Here are just a few examples:

- American Olympic athletes are often asked, "Are you happy with winning just a silver medal?" (Given her inspiring, courageous, and victorious comeback, it's amazing that Nancy Kerrigan was asked this question.)
- A crossword puzzle my wife and I were once working on asked for a five-letter word for "places second." Answer: "loses." (This may seem like an insignificant example, but it speaks volumes about how much our thinking has been affected by the "no place for second place" mentality.)
- High school and college coaches, even if their winning percentages are among the best in the record books, cannot escape the stigma of being a "loser" because of their "failures" to win the Big One. (Tragically, being this kind of "loser" often means *losing* your coaching job.)
- The "BuffaLLLLo BiLLLLs," as one sportswriter wrote after the 1994 Super Bowl, are four-time Super Bowl "LLLLosers." (Never mind the Bills' rare achievement of reaching the Super Bowl four seasons in a row!)
- A tee shirt has these words emblazoned on its back: "SECOND PLACE IS THE FIRST LOSER." (No comment needed. This example speaks for itself.)

The important point to stress here is that these less obvious examples of the "no place for second place" attitude can be just as harmful as those we read about or hear about on the news, especially in the long run. And in some cases, less may actually turn out to be *more*. As in more harmful. As in more destructive. Why?

Because often the things that hurt us the most are the little things that are not as obviously harmful to us. And these little things have a way, a very destructive way, of silently building up inside us and influencing our actions when we least expect it.

Like when we explode and begin screaming four-letter words at an umpire. Like when we take a swing at an opposing player's head. Like when we begin thinking that breaking "minor" rules isn't such a big deal. Like when we get in the habit of defending our unsportsmanlike actions by saying "everyone else does it." Like when we say things that make athletes or coaches feel that their self-worth depends entirely on their win-loss percentages. Like when our athletic successes begin to make us look down on other people who aren't as "good" as we are.

Little things can—and do—add up to very big things. Small amounts of "no place for second place" pollution can add up to lethal amounts of "no place for second place" pollution.

That's the reality of this #1 pollutant.

It can work as harmfully in small, less obvious amounts as it does in large, highly publicized amounts. It is an equal opportunity pollutant that contaminates sports, all the way from the big leagues down to the little league.

So when it comes to finding bad air, we need not look as far as the multimillion-dollar contests we watch on our TVs. We may need only to look as far as our local gyms and playing fields.

Or our own backyards, for that matter.

The #1 Polluter: The Best Reality Check Is a Gut Check

Now to nail down our sportsmanship reality check.

Chapter 2 asked about the extent of unsportsmanlike pollution, and chapter 3 asked about the game's #1 pollutant, but the single most important question still remains:

Who is most responsible for this unsportsmanlike pollution?

You see, we can talk about unsportsmanlike pollution in the abstract, as if it had a life of its own, but that wouldn't be very realistic. The fact is, this pollution has no life of its own. Pollutants like the "no place for second place" attitude have no life apart from *someone's* life. No attitude is an attitude apart from *someone's* attitude. There's no doubt that it's much easier and much more comfortable for us to talk about it abstractly, but what we're looking for here is reality, not comfort.

As all great coaches and athletes know, talking in the abstract never made anyone great. Nor did being comfortable. If you want to be the best you can be, then you have to be willing to pay a price. And you have to be realistic about that price, because it is most often paid in terms of discomfort, even pain.

No pain, no gain.

The same thing is true about success in cleaning up unsportsmanlike pollution. If we really care about cleaning it up, the first thing we have to do is be very realistic about it and be willing to pay a price.

So who is this *someone* who is most responsible for unsportsmanlike pollution?

The reality—and the price to be paid—is that the answer to this question ultimately requires each of us to look in the mirror. If we are realistic and honest with ourselves, we'll see that the answer can't primarily be in terms of someone else but has to be in terms of *this* someone.

Me.

Not in terms of him and his, her and hers, them and theirs, but in terms of *me* and *mine.*

It's fair to say that many of us tend to think of *other* athletes, coaches, and fans as the #1 polluters of the game, especially those athletes, coaches, and fans who do "really bad" things that are widely publicized.

But the opposite may be true: If I'm bending the rules, if I'm "only" breaking "minor" rules, if I'm shouting obscenities at game officials, if I'm talking trash to my opponents, if I'm a sore loser, if I'm doing it because everyone else does it—in short, if I think and act like second place is no place, then *I* am doing plenty of polluting myself. It may not be covered in the news, but it's the same destructive pollution nonetheless.

The reality is ironic. On the one hand, it's all too easy for me to see how someone else's "no place for second place" attitude is polluting the game but it's not always easy for me to see how my own "no place for second place" attitude is polluting the game.

On the other hand, it's all too easy for me to do something about my own "no place for second place" attitude but there's not much I can do about someone else's.

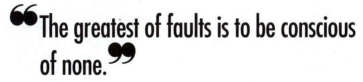

"The greatest of faults is to be conscious of none."

Thomas Carlyle

The buck ultimately stops with *me*. With *my* attitude. With my character.

In the long run, it won't do any good for us to point the finger at someone else. There's not much any of us can do about someone else's attitude and behavior. And all the new rules we can create won't go very far in cleaning up the unsportsmanlike pollution.

The best thing I can do to help clean up the unsportsmanlike pollution is to take care of *my* own character.

In the long run, *my* character is everything.

Sportsmanship and Ethics:

Two Sides of the Same Coin

First Things First

A true story: I was having a long lunch one sunny October afternoon with P. J. Carlesimo, then Seton Hall University's head basketball coach (now head coach of the National Basketball Association's Portland Trailblazers). We were both in Charlotte, North Carolina, attending the first Issues Summit, a conference sponsored by the National Association of Basketball Coaches, an association of nearly five thousand high school and college basketball coaches.

The NABC had organized this mega-conference in order to address several critical issues facing college sports, especially college basketball. Carlesimo and I had been invited to speak during a session on ethics, sportsmanship, and fair play issues.

During our lunch, Coach Carlesimo and I were strategizing about the best way to present these issues the following morning to several hundred basketball coaches and athletics administrators. After patiently listening to me talk in some detail about the connection between sportsmanship and ethics, Coach Carlesimo stopped me and said, "Look, Doc, I know you teach and write a lot about ethics, and I see what you're saying about how sportsmanship and ethics ultimately go hand in hand. But I'm telling you, Doc, if you get in front of all those coaches tomorrow and talk about 'ethics this' and 'ethics that,' a lot of them will probably end up tuning you out."

"Why do you think that, Coach?" I asked.

"I don't know exactly, but I think a lot of people may not associate sportsmanship with ethics. It's like sportsmanship is one thing, and they're comfortable talking about it because it's a sports thing. But to many people, ethics seems like something else, something more subjective, more like personal opinion. I think that may be why some people automatically become defensive or intimidated with ethics talk."

"But the fact is that ethics and sportsmanship do go hand in hand, Coach!"

"I know, Doc, I know," he replied. "All I'm saying is that before you can make your most important points about this thing called ethics, one of your first and biggest jobs will be to get people to see that connection. Otherwise, you may end up just spinning your wheels."

Leave it to a great coach to give great strategic advice. His advice not only served me well the following morning but has served me well ever since.

Two Sides of the Same Coin

It's important for me to point out that I'm not writing about sportsmanship and ethics together here simply because—as someone might assume—I enjoy sports and I teach courses in ethics. It's not as though they're completely different interests that I happen to be combining in this book.

On the contrary, the fact of the matter is that no one can write or talk about sportsmanship separately from ethics.

Sportsmanship is a big deal because ethics is a big deal.
If ethics isn't a big deal, sportsmanship isn't a big deal.

That's the bottom line about the connection between sportsmanship and ethics. And it really is that simple.

Think about it this way: What do we mean when we say, "She is a very ethical person," or "He was unethical when he did that"? By the first statement we usually mean that someone is a good person, that she has character, that she is a person of integrity, or even that she is a good role model. By the second statement we usually mean that someone's action was wrong, that it wasn't fair or honest or respectful or according to the rules—something like that.

The upshot is that when we talk about "ethics," we're usually talking about one or both of two important things: the kind of person someone is—his or her *character*—and someone's *actions*. So from now on we'll use this general definition for ethics:

Ethics is a matter of
being good (character) and doing right (action).

(We're going to look more closely at character and action and the connection between them in chapters 8–14, but for now we'll skip some of the details so that we can go ahead and get a handle on the connection between ethics and sportsmanship.)

Notice what happens when we ask the same sort of questions about sportsmanship that we just did about ethics: What do we usually mean when we say, "That coach is the epitome of sportsmanship," or "That athlete was very unsportsmanlike"?

The first statement, of course, points to a coach's good character. It says that a certain coach is the kind of person who characteristically does the sportsmanlike thing—the right thing. The second statement suggests that a particular athlete displayed some sort of unsportsmanlike behavior. The athlete might have fouled an opponent unnecessarily hard, shoved an umpire, used illegal drugs to gain a competitive advantage, or unfairly criticized teammates in public—something like that.

As with ethics, when we talk about "sportsmanship," we are talking about someone's character and actions, but specifically in the context of sports. So we'll use this general definition for sportsmanship:

Sportsmanship is a matter of
being good (character) and doing right (action) in sports.

66Good sportsmanship is not picking up lost golf balls while they are still rolling.99
Mark Twain

Given these two definitions, we see a connection between sportsmanship and ethics, that they both involve character and action—but so what? Why do they necessarily go hand in hand?

We can get to the heart of this connection by asking one more question: How many unsportsmanlike acts can you think of that would not be called unethical? In other words, if unethical acts are wrong because they are unfair, dishonest, disrespectful, or against the rules, how many unsportsmanlike acts can you think of that aren't wrong for the very same reasons?

Precisely *why* are unsportsmanlike acts wrong or bad?

Here's the point: The majority of acts that we consider bad in sports and call "unsportsmanlike" are bad precisely because they are unfair, dishonest, disrespectful, or against the rules. They are unsportsmanlike *because they are unethical.*

In most cases—and especially in the most important ones—sportsmanship and ethics turn out to be two sides of the same coin. That coin represents our standards of right and wrong, of good and bad, of fairness and unfairness, of honesty and dishonesty, of respect and disrespect, of following and breaking the rules, among other things.

Notice that it ultimately makes no difference whether we are talking about sports or not. Most of the acts we call unsportsmanlike are going to be wrong or bad outside the sports arena as well. The same goes for sportsmanlike acts.

A cheater is a cheater. An act of respect is an act of respect. Breaking a rule is breaking a rule. A good role model is a good role model.

So, when all is said and done, we could say that "sportsmanship" is the sports world's all-encompassing word for "ethics." That being sportsmanlike is being ethical in sports. That being unsportsmanlike is being unethical in sports.

And we can better appreciate why calling someone unsportsmanlike can be just as serious as calling someone unethical; why describing someone as sportsmanlike can be just as complimentary as describing someone as a very ethical person.

We can also better appreciate why there's no concept or value more important to sports than sportsmanship. It's our foundation, our starting point. It gives us our very best reason to play fairly, to show respect to opponents and officials, and to follow the rules—because all that is the right thing to do. The *ethical* thing.

With sportsmanship, we see that there's simply no escaping the ethical dimension of sports.

Without it, the game's over.

We're in the Same Ballpark

Coach Carlesimo made an important point when he said that many people seem to be more comfortable talking about "sportsmanship" than about "ethics."

Those of us who teach, speak, and write regularly about ethics have learned this all too well. I've learned, for instance, that when someone introduces me by saying something like "he teaches ethics," or "he is an ethicist," it can be one of the all-time great conversation stoppers. (I cringe any time I'm introduced as an "ethicist." To me, that sounds like I'm a laboratory doctor who's about to perform ethical surgery on unwitting, helpless patients. Don't ask me why.)

It's true that sometimes we don't know quite what to expect or what to think when the subject of ethics is brought up. Needless to say, "ethics" can be one of those red-flag words that automatically either puts us on the defensive or intimidates us, or both. Often we're not sure whether someone is getting ready to lecture us or preach at us or what.

These reactions are understandable, especially given a prevalent impression these days that someone speaking about ethics is just giving a very personal opinion about very controversial issues. For many, "ethics" has come to mean intense controversy. Not much more, not much less. Just an endless war of personal opinions.

But is it?

The first thing that needs to be said is that ethics can undoubtedly be controversial at times. And on any controversial issue we'll all certainly have our own opinions.

However, and this is extremely important, the impression that ethics is completely a matter of opinion and controversy is *wrong,* not to mention potentially dangerous. (Excuse the blunt language, but this is a point that's too important to be anything but straightforward about.)

What I want to emphasize here—and throughout this book— is that much of what ethics concerns is uncontroversial. In many ways, basic matters of character and action are as universal as air and as solid as diamonds; there is actually much more agreement about ethics than many of us may realize. It's crucial that we not only recognize this consensus and keep it in sight, but that we continue to act on it—as individuals, groups, teams, communities, leagues, societies.

Think about it: Don't we all agree that we should be the kind of people who are fair? Who are honest? Who are respectful? Who are responsible? Who generally follow the rules?

Don't we all agree that as competitors we should be sportsmanlike? Should play fairly? Should play by the rules?

"OK, OK," you might be thinking, "I get your point. But don't we disagree at times about exactly what is fair and honest and respectful?"

Of course we do—at times.

But notice two particular points. First, while we indeed have our differences of opinion at times about matters of character and action, we don't disagree *most* of the time. For example, we might disagree about whether a certain coach was sportsmanlike during a heated exchange with a referee, but we will agree that a coach *should* be

66 The moment we break faith with one another, the sea engulfs us and the light goes out. 99

James Baldwin

---

sportsmanlike when talking with a referee and that an act like threatening or assaulting a referee is absolutely *not* sportsmanlike.

Second, the fact that we disagree at times about precisely what is fair or respectful or sportsmanlike does not change the fact that we agree we should be the kind of people who are fair and honest and sportsmanlike. If you're still not completely convinced, think about what it would mean if there truly were not widespread agreement about ethics, about basic matters of character and action. If this were the case, we wouldn't be able to play our games. In fact, there probably wouldn't be any games to play! The same goes for society itself. Our games, and our society, ultimately depend on a number of basic ethical values, such as trust, fairness, honesty, respect for others, and respect for rules. Without these, games and society cannot function.

But, of course, our games and our society continue to function—far from perfectly, but they do function. And sometimes they function quite well.

The big problem is that we can fall into a trap of focusing so much on our disagreements that we lose sight of just how much we actually agree on when it comes to ethics and sportsmanship. Maybe it's cynicism and negativity at work again. Maybe it's something else. But the fact is, most of the time we're in the same ballpark when it comes to basic issues of character and action.

Part of what it's going to take to clean up the unsportmanlike pollution in our sports is *to appreciate just how much we agree on what clean air, as well as bad air, looks and feels like.* Generally speaking, most of us have a good idea of what it is to breathe clean or polluted air.

It's also going to take our best effort *to show others how important it is to welcome and promote discussion about sportsmanship, including "ethics" or "sports ethics," instead of being defensive or intimidated by these issues.* We can go a long way in doing this by proactively emphasizing our fundamental areas of agreement. Many times it's just a matter of calmly reminding each other of those basic values we share about having good character and doing the right thing.

Those shared values make ballparks possible. They make them *our* ballparks. And they make games possible there.

Make no mistake about it: Without them, we have no games. We don't even have a ballpark.

Character:
The Heart of the Matter

A Coach of Character

When it comes to talking about character, especially about building character, few expressions come to mind as quickly as the time-honored "sport builds character."

There are countless past and present athletes—including U.S. presidents such as Gerald Ford—who credit their coaches with helping them learn firsthand the profound significance of that expression. You may very well be one of these countless athletes.

I've often said that athletic coaches shaped my character as profoundly as anyone else—with the exception of my parents, of course, and a minister.

Of the many coaches I'm indebted to, one stands out above all the others, a coach to whom I can never repay my debt. A coach who has not only helped shape my character but who has taught me much about the essence of character—about what it is, how it is developed, what it can be, and how it is *everything.*

That coach, Mr. Tae Wae Haw, my tae kwon do instructor of more than ten years, is the one to whom I have dedicated this book.

In the tradition of all great coaches, Mr. Haw coaches and teaches about character more than anything else. He is a master at teaching athletic skills—such as the skills of self-defense—but his greatest mastery lies in his dedication and ability to teach skills of character.

It took me quite a while, long after I had earned my first-degree black belt, to realize that what Mr. Haw is all about—what he is really after—is personal character. And I don't mean "character" in the abstract or in theory. His approach to teaching and coaching is always practical, sometimes painfully practical: The focus is on developing and honing specific strengths of character, facing up to and overcoming specific weaknesses of character.

He's the type of mentor par excellence who helps you learn the hard way about character what you thought you "knew" the easy way. And sometimes, lessons about character can be learned only the hard way.

Like the first time I got inadvertently kicked—kicked really hard—between the legs while sparring. Predictably, I fell to my knees and doubled over, grimacing in pain. All I remember is that next, in an instant, Mr. Haw picked me up from behind, made me stand up, and thundered, "Are you just going to stay down and cover your head like a frightened puppy after someone has attacked you on the street? Are you going to ask them, 'please wait a second so I can catch my breath'? You'll be dead!"

Then he immediately said in a "don't make me say it again" tone of voice: "Continue!"

I continued. For the life of me, I don't know how I was able to continue sparring, because it *did* hurt, and hurt badly. It was the kind of hurt that makes it hard to breathe, much less move. But I did continue—with Mr. Haw's help, of course.

Since he can read me so well, I have no doubt that Mr. Haw knew much more was involved than just the matter of working through the pain of getting hit. He knew that I was so afraid of getting hurt that I probably *was* going to get hurt unless I confronted that fear. It was a matter—a lesson—of overcoming fear and learning to exercise courage in the face of adversity.

It proved to be a defining moment for me—not so much in terms of self-defense but just in terms of *self*. In other words, in terms of my character.

Another time, Mr. Haw told me to use a small balloon to help perfect my punch. He told me to hang the balloon by a string at about face level, and to begin punching it. That's all he said.

For literally months and months I kept trying to figure out what the heck I was supposed to be learning from punching a balloon that weighed no more than a few feathers. After throwing countless thousands of punches at that blankety-blank balloon, I was still asking myself: Is it supposed to help me learn how to shift my weight better? Is it somehow supposed to help me focus the energy of my punches better? Am I supposed to learn how to break the balloon with a single punch? Am I supposed to learn how to make it bob up and down, and not sway, like a heavy bag does when punched correctly? And, finally, what *is* the deal with this stupid balloon?

Mr. Haw never answered any of those questions for me.

He knew, of course, that *eventually* I would answer them all for myself. And when I finally did come up with some answers, I realized that his balloon idea was meant more to correct a flaw in my character than one in my punch. Looking back, I appreciate more than ever how Mr. Haw was helping me deal with an impatience, an attitude that said, "If I can understand it right away, then I can be good at it right away." That "stupid" balloon taught me that if I wanted to become truly excellent at anything, then I had to do it over and over until it became second nature.

With many other lessons such as these, Mr. Haw helped teach me that personal character is where it's at. He taught me

- that character is built more than built-in
- that if you want to truly learn to master anything, you must first learn to master yourself
- that when it comes to building good character—in or out of the competitive arena—there is no substitute for sweat, for hard work, for practice
- that character is what you are when no one's looking
- that character is what you are when everyone's looking
- that success or excellence or winning, whatever you want to call it, isn't about victories or defeats; isn't about trophies, medals, or ribbons; isn't about fame or fortune; isn't about statistics

It's about *what you are and what you do with what you are.* It's about *personal character.*

❝The final forming of a person's character lies in their own hands.❞

Anne Frank

Getting "Ethical"
from "Athletic"

Every so often, crucial points are unforgettably driven home in the smallest—and most unexpected—ways.

Like the time I was leading a discussion with a group of student athletes about the connection between athletic excellence and ethical excellence.

I had written two phrases on the blackboard: "Being Athletic" and "Being Ethical."

"What connection do you see between being athletic and being ethical?" I asked.

When no one jumped at the chance to answer, I proceeded to call on a member of the women's swimming team and a member of the men's tennis team, both of whom were obviously much more interested in each other that day than in the topic of discussion.

Unsurprisingly, they were caught completely off guard.

The tennis player clearly had no idea what was going on in the discussion. He just shrugged his shoulders, cracked a smile, and said with a red face, "I wish I knew."

Everyone laughed.

At that point everyone, including myself, couldn't wait to hear how the swimmer was going to respond. A tough-nosed competitor in more ways than one, she was not easily embarrassed and she hardly ever backed away from a challenge. And she was hardly ever at a loss for words—especially very funny ones.

She stared at the blackboard for several seconds, then said in a tone of voice that was both dramatic and sarcastic, "I don't see much of anything, to tell you the truth. The only thing I can see is that if you rearrange the letters of 'athletic,' you get the word 'ethical'—with an extra 't' left over."

She paused as all of us burst out laughing. Then, to top it off, she added, "But if we were to let the extra 't' stand for 'talent,' I guess we could conclude that they both take talent. So there you go! That's the connection—they both take talent!"

We laughed even louder.

She had hit a home run—but not necessarily for the reason you might think.

Of course, the quick-witted swimmer had proved once again that she was up to a challenge and that she thought very well on her feet, and we all got a big laugh out of her response. But, truth be told, she had hit a home run not because her response was entertaining but because it was *right*. As in *right on target*.

She had unexpectedly taken the class to the heart of my question about athletic excellence and ethical excellence—even if at that moment she and the rest of the class did not realize it. And the way she went about doing it was more effective than anything I could have told them that afternoon. It might seem insignificant, but the way she led the group to think of "athletic" as an anagram of "ethical," with an extra "t" for "talent," was nothing short of intuitive genius—at least as far as I was concerned.

Why was it intuitive genius? Because what I had been trying to aim the discussion toward was *character*. In other words, what I had been trying to drive home about the connection between athletic and ethical excellence was that both ultimately depend on character.

And talent is at the very center of character.

Out of nowhere, the inattentive swimmer had hit the bull's-eye of my question, dead center.

A Bundle of Strengths and Weaknesses

If you thought you were left hanging at the end of chapter 9, you were right.

So did that group of student athletes when I ended my discussion with them the same way, by saying—with no further explanation—that talent is at the very center of character. (You know how teachers like doing that sort of thing when we want to keep our students' intellectual wheels turning.)

So what's the connection between talent and character? And what does this connection have to do with the connection between athletic and ethical excellence?

This is one of those times when it can help to consult your dictionary, even though you already have a good idea of what certain commonly used words mean—words like "talent" and "character."

If you look up the word "talent," one of the first entries you'll find is one like this in *The American Heritage Dictionary*:

talent *n*. 1. A natural or acquired ability; aptitude.

In other words, to have talent is to have an ability that either (1) came naturally to you, or (2) was acquired through hard work, because it didn't come naturally to you.

When you look up the word "character," you'll likely find several entries. The ones that are most relevant here will read something like these:

character n. 1. The combination of qualities that distin
guishes one person, group, or thing from another. 2.
A distinguishing feature or attribute, as of an individual, a group, or a category. 3. Moral or ethical
strength. 4. A description of a person's attributes,
traits, and abilities.

In definition four—"moral and ethical strength"—and especially
in the last word of the last definition—"abilities"—you can begin to
see the connection between talent and character. It's simply this:
*Character will always involve having or developing certain kinds
of talents.*

The point isn't that talent is all there is to character. But we
can be sure that at the very center of our own personal character
there will always be these two core ideas. First, there will be the idea
of *what we're good at*—our strengths, our skills, our abilities. Some
of these abilities come naturally to us, some of them don't.

And since some of these abilities don't come naturally, there
will also always be the idea of *what we're not so good at*—our
weaknesses, our faults, our inabilities. In other words, there will
also be those abilities that we don't have or at least haven't yet mas-
tered. They're the ones we are attempting to or need to develop.

Thus, we can see how personal character will always involve
both what we're good at and what we're not good at, our abilities
and our inabilities, our strengths and our weaknesses.

We seldom talk, of course, in terms of "talents of character" or of
"abilities of character." We typically use the words "talent" and "ability" to describe particular skills that someone has—as in "she is very
talented at gymnastics" or "he has tremendous athletic ability."

But we do frequently talk in terms of "strengths" of character
and "weaknesses" of character, which more often than not imply
strong and weak *abilities* of character (like when a fan says, "One
of our coach's greatest strengths is her ability to withstand criti-
cism during a losing season"). And the related expression we probably use more than any other—"character traits"—is most often
used in the same way: to describe someone's abilities or inabilities
to be or to act one way rather than another (like when a football
coach says, "My quarterback's number-one character trait is his
ability to keep his poise under pressure").

Enough of the definitional stuff. What does all of this have to do with the connection between athletic excellence and ethical excellence? Everything.

As in—you guessed it—*character is everything.*

It's easy, of course, to see how character is necessary for athletic excellence. If someone said to you, "It takes a lot of character to be a winner" or "Athletic success ultimately boils down to your character," they wouldn't be telling you anything you didn't already know.

But the same principle about character applies to ethical excellence as well.

When you think of personal character as a bundle of talents and talents-to-be, of abilities and inabilities, of strengths and weaknesses, you can see that becoming a good athlete and becoming a good person are not so different.

They're not so different because they both ultimately depend on personal character—on our own personal bundle of strengths and weaknesses. They both depend on playing to our strengths and facing up to our weaknesses. They both depend on exercising our natural abilities and developing our not-so-natural abilities.

And it's of great importance that we're not talking about two different bundles that make up personal character. It's not as though we

---

66You cannot attain and maintain physical condition unless you are morally and mentally conditioned. I tell my players that our team condition depends on two factors — how hard they work on the floor during practice and how well they behave between practices.**99**

John Wooden

have one character as a good athlete and another character as a good person. We may show traits of character when playing sports that we normally don't show when off the field or off the court, but it's the *same* personal character. Here's the bottom line:

The character that

gets you out of that bottom-of-the-ninth jam,
makes it possible for you to develop better technique,
sees you through that losing season,
enables you to play like you've never played before,
holds you up while you endure those killer, never-ending drills of
      pre-season training,
helps you overcome the disappointment of a season-ending injury,
makes you run faster, jump higher, throw farther, swim faster, hit
      better,
encourages you to dig a little deeper during overtime,
helps you carry your team to the championship,
and ultimately earns you MVP or all-state or all-American honors,

is the very same character that

pushes you to shake your opponent's hand when you don't
      want to,
makes you treat officials, referees, and umpires with respect,
helps you follow the rules,
makes you gracious in defeat,
encourages you to act like a good role model,
keeps you from taking a cheap shot at your opponent,
helps you resist the temptation to use performance-enhancing
      drugs,
helps you see your way out of ethical dilemmas,
prevents you from cheating,

and, in a nutshell,

makes you do the right thing.
The ethical thing.
The sportsmanlike thing.

A Test of Character

While this won't be a particularly uplifting story, it will take us to the heart of sportsmanship and ethics. And that's exactly what we're after here, *the heart of the matter*.

I'll call him "A. J."

A. J. was a standout, blue-chip athlete who enrolled in my sports ethics seminar at Pepperdine University during his first semester in college.

I especially want you to understand the main reason he didn't make it to his second semester.

As his teacher and freshman adviser, I had come to like A. J. a lot; so had his classmates. He was very easy to like. Though by nature quiet and shy, he eventually became one of the class's favorite personalities. He got along well with everyone and had a smile and a laugh that, when expressed, were very contagious.

I vividly remember when my wife, Jeannine, and I invited A. J. and the 20 other freshman student athletes in that class over to our house for dinner. One of the reasons I remember that evening so well is that the class voted to schedule the dinner on the night of the first championship boxing match between Riddick Bowe and Evander Holyfield.

Everyone chipped in a couple of dollars to cover the cost of the pay-per-view telecast. Some of the students wanted to watch the fight because they liked boxing, while others wanted to use the high-profile fight to begin discussing the ethical issues of violence in sports (one of the course's topics).

It became clear right after the opening bell that A. J. was a huge Bowe fan. It also became clear that the usually reserved A. J. was going to be the life of this party. He was comically entertaining, rattling off Dick Vitale-like color commentary one minute and screaming encouragement as though he were Bowe's cornerman the next.

Bowe won that fight, of course, and A. J. acted like he had won as well. He basked in the glory of Bowe's victory, providing all of us with post-fight hilarity.

A. J. was the last one to leave our house that evening.

For the first time, I had gotten a good sense of just how likable, polite, and spirited A. J. was. He was definitely someone I would have wanted to get to know better.

I wish I had. Perhaps he would have made it to his second semester and beyond.

As a teacher and as an academic adviser, I believe it's important to get to know my student athlete advisees as early as possible. And by "get to know" I mean learn about both their academic abilities and their character makeup. That way, I can counsel them as wisely and effectively as possible for their college careers and beyond.

In all of life, early preparation is crucial to long-term success. And the very demanding challenge of being a student athlete—whether in high school or college—is certainly no exception to that rule. (If you are or have been a student athlete, you know exactly what I'm talking about.)

All I knew of A. J. up to that point, two months or so into the semester, was that he was a highly recruited basketball player from a big city in another state. Blessed with a strong body, a soft shooting touch, great jumping ability, and a hard-nosed competitive attitude, he had the potential to become a brilliant impact player—in his freshman season, no less.

Shortly after the Bowe-Holyfield outing, I visited A. J.'s coach to learn more about him, especially about more than just his athletic skills.

Coach told me about A. J.'s background, his family, as well as his strengths and weaknesses on and off the court. It was obvious to me from his thoughtful descriptions that Coach really cared about A. J.

❝Character is destiny.❞
Heraclitus

Of all the things Coach told me about A. J., one description stood out. Right before I got up to leave his office, he had concluded our conversation by saying, "A. J. is a diamond in the rough."

A diamond in the rough.

Though I knew—and had used—the expression many times myself, I was especially intrigued by the way Coach had used it to refer to A. J. Judging from the concerned, fatherly look on Coach's face, it was as if he was *feeling* the expression, not merely using it.

After a moment of awkward silence, I asked, "What'd you mean by that, Coach?"

"Well, A. J. has more than enough raw athleticism to become a very, very good ballplayer," he said. "But to tell you the truth, I'm not sure that he has the character to become a brilliant diamond. I guess when I used the expression 'a diamond in the rough,' I was thinking more of his rough character than his rough basketball skills."

Tragically, his words turned out to be prophetic.

Between semesters, while most students were at home on Christmas break, A. J. and another student broke into some dorm rooms and stole several hundred dollars worth of stereo equipment.

They were caught.

I was shocked. I really was. I wouldn't have—couldn't have—predicted it.

I remember thinking when I read in a local newspaper about the theft and A. J.'s dismissal from school: "A. J., how could you do such a ridiculous thing? You took my sports ethics—*ethics!*—class, for crying out loud!"

In retrospect, I realize that I reacted that way not simply because I liked A. J.; I also reacted that way because of wounded pride—my teaching pride.

After all, A. J. *had taken* my sports ethics course, and he *had passed it*—a course that dealt all semester with issues of right and wrong and good and bad. "Hadn't he learned anything?" I remember asking myself over and over.

I know he'd learned something. He had to have learned something: He had passed the course, hadn't he?

In fact, not only did he pass the course but the grade he received on his final exam was something A. J. could be proud of—it was his best of the semester.

When all was said and done, however, grades were beside the point. As much as I might hate to admit it, even my sports ethics course was beside the point. Whether he passed a certain test or passed a certain course—even an *ethics* course—was not the issue.

The issue was another kind of test, the most important test of all: The *character* test.

A. J. had failed that test.

Having the Character to Do the Right Thing

The moral of A. J.'s story is not that we should dwell on his—or anyone else's—failures. Far from it. Nor is it that someone like A. J. is a bad person for failing any single test of character. He's *not,* and it's doubtful that any of us would want to be judged by such a strict, one-strike-and-you're-out ethical standard.

As could be said of so many of us, A. J. is basically a very good person with a very big heart who unfortunately made a very big mistake.

And as could be said of most of us, his mistake was made knowing full well that what he was doing was wrong. That's the moral to the story.

A. J.'s story helps drive home this simple yet crucial point about sportsmanship and ethics: More than anything else, doing the right thing involves *having the character to do the right thing.* In other words, it's mostly about having the will, the courage, and the guts to do what is right.

The will, courage, and guts—the *character*—more than anything else.

Anything.

Even more than *knowing* the right thing.

Why? For this simple reason: When it comes to doing the right thing, we usually already know what the right thing to do is.

Remember the commonly used expression, "You should have known better" (the one we've all probably had said to us more times than we care to remember!)? If we think long and hard enough about it, we'll probably discover that we usually *do* know better when it comes to being sportsmanlike and being ethical.

That's why character is *the heart and soul of sportsmanship and ethics.*

Most of the time, it's not as though we don't know that we shouldn't break the rules, that we should treat the referees with respect, that we shouldn't use drugs, that we should shake our opponent's hand, that we shouldn't fight with the visiting fans, that we should play fairly, that we shouldn't intentionally hurt anyone, that we should be a team player, and that we shouldn't be a poor loser.

Most of the time, we know the difference between what we should and shouldn't do. Between what is sportsmanlike and what is unsportsmanlike. Between what is ethical and unethical. Between what is right and wrong.

Not always, but most of the time.

There is no doubt that we're occasionally faced with difficult ethical situations in which we truly don't know what the right thing to do is. Some of us will face more of these situations than others.

These situations—what we often call "ethical dilemmas"—can be very tough, and sometimes the best we can do is *do the best we can do under the circumstances.* Sometimes we may have to make a decision on the spur of the moment, when we don't have enough time to sort out all the pros and cons. Sometimes, with a little advice from a friend or with plenty of time to think the whole thing over on our own, we can decide exactly what we should do.

But we're focusing primarily on what happens most of the time, because, on a day-to-day or game-to-game basis, uncertainty over the right thing to do is not usually the problem. (Don't think

---

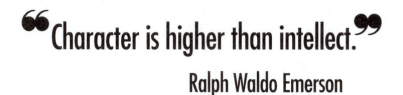

❝Character is higher than intellect.❞

Ralph Waldo Emerson

you're being left completely in the dark about the difficult situations we can face: I offer some concrete suggestions on how to deal with them in "A Three-Point Sportmanship Checklist" near the end of the book.)

Most of the time, if there's any problem with being ethical or being sportsmanlike, it will be a problem of *what we're made of* more than *what we know.*

Of *character* more than *knowledge.*

Thus, most of the time, the single most important question to ask ourselves is:

> Do I have the will, the courage, and
> the guts—the character—
> to do the right thing?

That's the heart-of-the-matter question for sportsmanship and ethics, and it's one that you and only you can ultimately answer. I can tell you some things about the question, like how important it is, but only *you* can answer it.

One final note to preclude any misunderstanding about this chapter's basic point: What you know is obviously very important. And increasing your knowledge can undoubtedly help you become a better person.

But when all is said and done, the basic point remains: Doing the right thing and being a good person begin and end with your personal character—no matter what your IQ is, no matter how many academic degrees you have, no matter how many "ethics" courses you may have taken or taught.

To make this all-important point as strongly as possible, allow me to state it in this personal way: The fact that I have a doctorate in ethics, that I may in some sense "know" the great ethical theories well, and that I regularly teach courses in ethics and moral education does not say anything about how good I am as a person.

Just because a person knows a lot about something, even about ethics, does not mean that person is ethical.

As my parents often reminded me, *being smart does not necessarily mean being good.*

Or, as many wise men and women have said in times past, *knowledge without character is worthless at best and evil at worst.*

The test for doing the right thing and being a good person is almost always going to be a character test—a *never-ending* character test.

When "Just Doing It" Is Hard

Doing the right thing—the ethical thing—isn't always easy. Sometimes it's very hard. And most of us would be less than honest if we said otherwise.

As I mentioned in the last chapter, doing the right thing can be hard because we really don't know what to do.

But most of the time we really *do* know. So why in the world is it so difficult at times to "just do it" if we already know what we should do?

There's no great mystery here. And since there's not, allow me to talk like a no-nonsense coach and get right to the point: If there's a problem at times with being sportsmanlike, it ultimately resides in each of us.

In *me.* In *my own* personal character.

And it's usually because of something going on in our gut and not in our head. What's going on at gut level is often an intense one-on-one competition between

What I *ought* to do

vs.

What I *want* to do

or

How I *feel* at the moment
or
What I would *like* to happen
or
What I *fear* might happen to me

But describing it this way is still a little too abstract, still a little too comfortable—at least as far as this no-nonsense "coach" is concerned. Here's what these one-on-one competitions of the gut actually end up looking—and *feeling*—like:

I really should shake my opponent's hand
vs.
The last thing I want to do is shake my opponent's hand

I ought to tell the truth about what happened
vs.
I'm afraid of what'll happen if I tell the truth

I shouldn't pick a fight with my opponent
vs.
I'd like to rearrange my opponent's face

I shouldn't use drugs
vs.
I want to win no matter what it takes

I shouldn't yell four-letter words at the referee
vs.
I'm royally ticked off at that referee for making such a bad call

I shouldn't break this rule
vs.
If I want to keep up with the competition, I've got to break this rule

It's internal struggles such as these within each of us that can make doing the right thing so hard at times.

Now think about it: What's ultimately going to decide the outcome of these internal struggles? What's ultimately going to make the difference in determining whether you do the sportsmanlike thing or not?

It's the same thing that ultimately makes the difference in the final minutes of a very close game: The strengths—and weaknesses—of *your own personal character.*

That's the hard truth of the matter. We can talk at great length about the pressures, about the temptations, about how he did this and she did that, about how all the other teams do it, about how they were going to do this and they weren't going to do that, about how stressed out we are, about any number of other things, but even if all these are *true,* they may be beside the point when it comes to sportsmanship and ethics. Much of the time they turn out to be nothing but a bunch of flimsy excuses.

Please don't infer that I'm pointing any fingers. Believe me, I've got my own bag of ready-to-use excuses and rationalizations with which I'm continually dealing.

All I'm trying to emphasize is that when it comes to doing the right thing, the sportsmanlike thing, the buck stops with *me* and *my own* personal character. *My* actions are *my* responsibility. *I* and *I* alone am responsible for the actions that flow from *my* character.

Notice that, in the list of internal struggles I just gave, nothing like the following was included:

I shouldn't break this rule
vs.
Everyone else is breaking this rule

Do you know why? The reason is important: We don't, ultimately, break rules because everyone else is breaking them. Nor can we ever really blame anyone else when we break rules. We break rules primarily because of something we *want:* Because we *want* to win. Or because we *want* to succeed. Or because we *want* to be famous. Or because we *want* to be accepted. It's usually for something we *want.* And that means breaking rules is still going to be something for which my own character is ultimately and solely responsible.

Therefore, when it comes to doing something like breaking rules, the real struggle is *not* between us and everyone else—or *anyone else,* for that matter. The real struggle is an internal one between *what I should do* and *what I want;* in other words, between

I should follow the rules
vs.
I want to win so badly that I will break the rules

The same goes for any kind of cheating.

More often than not, what *everyone else is doing* will be irrelevant when it comes to *doing what is right*. It doesn't really matter what your opponents are doing or saying; what your teammates and coaches are doing or saying; what the fans and the media are doing or saying; what *anyone* is doing or saying.

All that matters is what you are, and what you do and say because of what you are.

The bottom line: *I am ultimately responsible for my character and the actions flowing from my character because absolutely no one can make me do something against my will that I know is wrong.*

---

66 People of character don't allow the environment to dictate their style. 99
Lucille Kallen

Becoming Good at
"Just Doing It"

To achieve success, whatever the job we have, we must pay a price for success. It's like anything worthwhile. It has a price. You have to pay the price to win and you have to pay the price to get to the point where success is possible. Most important, you must pay the price to stay there. Success is not a 'sometimes' thing. In other words, you don't do what is right once in a while, but all the time. Success is a habit. Winning is a habit. . . .Unfortunately, so is losing.

Vince Lombardi

Coach Lombardi couldn't have said it better if he had been talking specifically about sportsmanship and ethics.

Success and winning *are* habits. Excellence is a habit.

Success, winning, and excellence in *anything* are habits.

And it's important for us to see and to keep in mind that this "habit principle" applies as much to

> *success in becoming a great person*
> *who always does the sportsmanlike thing*

as it does to

> *success in becoming a great athlete*
> *who always does the MVP thing.*

Does this sound familiar? It should, because we've returned to where we began our discussion about character. We're back to square one: about how ethical excellence and athletic excellence both depend on our personal character—our own personal bundle of strengths and weaknesses. About how they both depend on playing to our strengths and facing up to our weaknesses. About how they both depend on exercising our natural abilities and developing our not-so-natural abilities.

In other words, they both depend on developing and maintaining *good habits.*

What's so important about developing good habits?

Well, you have to develop good habits to become really good at something—at least if you want to be really good at something *consistently.*

But here's a better way of looking at it: Why do you practice the same athletic skills and techniques over and over? Why do you hit, serve, catch, throw, shoot, or kick that ball thousands of times, to the point where you're wondering why you're even doing it? Why do you spend countless hours running, jumping, swimming, riding, or lifting until you're completely exhausted? Why do you run those plays over and over until you're sick of them?

Yes, part of it is because "coach tells me to!" But why does your coach tell you to do it over and over?

So that your skills and techniques become *second nature.*

So that they become *automatic.*

So that they become such *ingrained habits* that most of the time you don't have to think about what you're doing.

You just do it.

And you do it well—automatically, naturally.

That's it.

That's exactly what Coach Lombardi meant.

That's the key to being successful. To being a winner.

"Character is a victory, not a gift."

Anonymous

To being excellent in anything. Especially in ethics and sportsmanship.

Just as our goal in sports is to

become a truly great athlete who
naturally and consistently does the MVP thing,

our goal in ethics and sportsmanship should be to

become a truly great person who
naturally and consistently does the sportsmanlike thing.

In both cases, the goal we're striving for is having character that lets us do the right thing naturally and consistently. In the first case, it's a matter of doing the right *athletic* thing naturally and consistently; in the second, of doing the right *ethical* thing naturally and consistently.

And now we can begin to see the ultimate solution for those times when being sportsmanlike can be so hard. For those times when the gut is a battleground between *what I ought to do* and *what I want to do.*

The ultimate solution is to develop good habits of character so that *what I ought to do* and *what I want to do* become teammates, not opponents. They work in harmony—naturally and consistently.

In other words, we should strive to develop good, strong habits of character so that *what I want to do* naturally and consistently follows *what I ought to do.*

But how can we get to the point where we naturally and consistently do the right thing, the sportsmanlike thing?

The first thing to mention here is that it's not as though most of us naturally and consistently do the wrong thing, the unsportsmanlike thing. My own opinion is that, most of the time, most athletes and coaches are trying their best to play the game in a sportsmanlike way. I can't prove it; it's just something I happen to believe based on my own experiences.

But none of us, of course, are perfect in character. To varying degrees, we're all "diamonds in the rough." There's always room for improvement in developing the kind of character that enables us to do the right thing naturally and consistently.

There's no magic formula for developing this kind of excellence in character, but it will always involve at least three things, the same three things required for athletic excellence:

1. The desire for excellence
2. The commitment to excellence
3. Practice, practice, practice!

First, if you don't have the desire to be excellent at something, you never will be. It's that simple. It's as true for ethical excellence as it is for athletic excellence. If you don't have the desire to strive for ethical excellence, you'll never reach it, no matter how much anyone else tries to help you. You've got to *want* it. Period.

Just remember that if there's a will, there's always a way. So let's resist the temptation to make lame excuses like "well, that's just the way I am." That may be the way I am, but that doesn't necessarily make it good or right. Think about it: Can you imagine yourself saying to your coach, who's just been criticizing you for your continual lack of hustle on defense, "Well, coach, I'm sorry, but there's not a lot I can do about it, it's just the way I am"? (I didn't think so.)

Second, your desire for ethical excellence must be accompanied by a genuine, heartfelt dedication to develop it. Like any kind of excellence, ethical excellence does not happen overnight. In fact, it happens over a whole lifetime. That's why it requires the kind of commitment that doesn't—and shouldn't—ever end.

Third, as with athletic excellence, you've got to practice doing the right thing over and over to get to the point where you do it naturally and consistently. This may need more emphasis than the first two points.

Why? Because while it's usually fairly obvious that good character requires personal desire and commitment to be good, and while it's fairly obvious that we need to practice hard to become really good at something like sports, it may not be so obvious that doing the ethical thing—naturally and consistently—requires the same kind of practice. The same kind of hard work. Of repetition. Of determined exercise. Of doing something over and over again until it becomes automatic.

In fact, that's exactly why each of us already possesses certain strengths of character—because someone very important in our lives encouraged us or *made* us do the right thing over and over until it became second nature. That's in large measure what becoming a good person is all about and why it never stops.

It's a never-ending matter of exercising our strengths of character and overcoming our weaknesses of character. It's a matter of exercising our natural ethical abilities and developing other not-so-natural ethical abilities.

Consider:

If you're a tennis player and you've got a weak backhand, what do you do?

If you're a basketball player and you're having trouble going to your left because your left hand is your nonshooting hand, what do you do?

If you're a baseball player and your batting average continues to suffer because you keep bailing out of the batter's box out of fear you might get hit by a pitch, what do you do?

If you're a volleyball player and your digs are just not digging, what do you do?

If you're a football player—a quarterback—and your passes are wobbling more than spiraling, what do you do?

Whatever kind of athlete you are, what do you do about a weakness in your game, especially when it's costing you games?

You practice it over and over until what was *weak* becomes *strong.*

So, putting two and two together here:

If you have a tendency to be quick-tempered, what do you do?

66 To enjoy the things we ought and to hate the things we ought has the greatest bearing on excellence of character. 99

Aristotle

If you find yourself regularly putting down other people, even your own teammates, what do you do?

If telling lies has become easy for you, what do you do?

If your attitude is making you act as if there's no place for second place, what do you do?

If bending—even breaking—the rules has become almost natural when the going gets tough, what do you do?

What *do* you do about weaknesses in your character, especially when they're getting you into some kind of trouble?

You guessed it: You practice doing *the right thing* repeatedly until what was *weak* is now *strong*. Until a specific weakness of character is transformed into a strength of character that naturally and consistently helps you do the right thing.

This point can't be emphasized enough: It's all about what you are and what you do with what you are. It's all about taking responsibility for what you are—and for what you do. It's about exercising your strengths of character and overcoming your weaknesses of character.

It's all about character.
That's the name of the game.
It's the name of the game we play.
And it's the name of the "game" we must live.

---

*Three characters can be found in a man
about to perform a good deed:
If he says, "I shall do it soon," his character is poor.
If he says, "I am ready to do it now," his character is of
average quality.
If he says, "I am doing it," his character is praiseworthy.*
—Hasidic saying

Role Models:
Getting Clear on the Concept

About a Certain Ad-itude

Open with the dead-serious, unsmiling face of pro basketball star
  Charles Barkley.
"I am not a role model."
Cut to a basketball gym, where a sweating Barkley is practicing by himself.
  He rebounds, then dribbles between his legs.
"I'm not paid to be a role model."
Rebound, dribble, more sweat.
"I am paid to wreak havoc on the basketball court."
More dribbles, more rebounds, more sweat.
"Parents should be role models."
More rebounds. Then a ferocious, two-handed slam dunk.
"Just because I can dunk a basketball doesn't mean I should raise
  your kids."

You knew that we couldn't talk about role models without mentioning this world-famous, thirty-second Nike commercial, right?

Say what you want about it, but this Nike ad helped get us thinking and talking about the important issue of athletes as role models.

While Barkley—and Nike—certainly took some heat for it—and some of that heat was understandable—in the long run the commercial served a good purpose. I didn't think so at first, but after noticing how much *constructive* discussion it was generating, I started seeing it in a different light.

❝Example is not the main thing in life – it is the only thing.❞

Albert Schweitzer

Besides, it's not as though Sir Charles's "ad-itude" was completely wrong. In certain respects, and especially on parents being role models, it was clearly right on target.

But many people, including me, had a great deal of trouble getting past that in-your-face opening line: "I am not a role model." Unsurprisingly, we had trouble with it because we didn't agree with it.

I hope you're not expecting me to start attacking Barkley's (or Nike's) character and motives for the "I am not a role model" statement, because I'm not going to. After all, if I'm going to practice what I preach about not making sweeping generalizations and not judging people in a way that I wouldn't want to be judged myself, then I need to be very, very careful about attacking anyone's character and motives—whether they are famous or not.

The issue of whether athletes are role models is an important one we definitely need to discuss, but we also need to keep in mind how easy it can be for discussion about this kind of issue to turn into a character assassination issue. The main reason is that it often can be all too easy for us to slide into a discussion where we begin making sweeping judgments about someone else's character—when the truth is we really don't know what we're talking about. And sometimes we can be guilty of assassinating someone's character without realizing what we're doing.

Any way you look at it, it's serious business.

And since discussing role models is serious business, we should keep in mind something like this: *We should try our best to be role models when discussing role models.*

In other words, if it gets to the point where we are asking whether someone else is a role model—and we all know that discussions about role models often get to that point—then we need to have the character to talk about someone else the way we would hope someone else would talk about us. Whether that someone else is a teammate, a coach, an opponent, or a professional athlete doesn't matter. The same Golden Rule applies.

If I still haven't made this point strongly enough, think about this sobering thought a minister once shared with me: *People never reveal their own character so clearly as when they describe someone else's character.* Talk about a powerful one-liner.

What we're going to do here is take the message of Nike's "I am not a role model" commercial at face value and see what we can learn from it about the issue of role models, *without* asking any questions about Barkley's character or about Nike's motives. What, then, are we to make of Sir Charles's ad-itude? Is he right in saying that he's not a role model? Are athletes role models or not?

Here's the short answer: It depends.

The answer depends on how we interpret the question.

Here's one important insight I've learned from discussing this type of question with different groups of athletes, coaches, parents, officials, sportswriters, fans, and others: When two people disagree about the answer to this kind of question, it's almost always because they're answering *different* questions. In other words, they're taking the same question very differently.

Some will take the question

> *Are athletes role models?*

to mean

> *Do athletes have a responsibility to be role models?*

Others will take the question

> *Are athletes role models?*

to mean

> *Should people CHOOSE athletes as their role models?*

❝Character builds slowly, but it can be torn down with incredible swiftness.❞

Faith Baldwin

Thus, it's helpful to remember that the answer to this important question of whether athletes are role models will usually depend on whether we're talking about

athletes being role models

or

choosing athletes as role models

When two people who disagree come to see that they are interpreting the question in these two different ways, they usually find out that they actually *agree* on the issue of athletes as role models, especially on this basic point: However you interpret the question, its answer will ultimately boil down to a matter of personal character.

Being a Role Model

To be or not to be?

That's not the question.

That's never the question when it comes to being a role model.

And that's why in an important sense Charles Barkley's "I am not a role model" statement is dead wrong. He most definitely *is* a role model.

It may sound as though I'm getting ready to speculate about Barkley's personal character when I said I wouldn't—but don't worry, I haven't and I won't.

I've said bluntly that Barkley is definitely a role model to help establish the first of two key points: In a very basic sense, asking whether *anyone* is a role model is like asking whether a ball is round.

If we're using the term *role model*—as we so often use it—to mean a person who sets an example for others, who influences others, whom other people learn from and imitate, then Barkley is obviously a role model. Just as all athletes and all coaches are role models.

Just as *every single one of us* is a role model.

In this basic sense, we—like Barkley—simply don't have a choice in the matter.

It's not as though we can decide *not to be* role models. We're role models whether we accept it or not, whether we like it or not, and whether we realize it or not. We simply can't escape it.

Therefore, let's make sure we're not thinking primarily of role models in terms of professional athletes like Charles Barkley.

A great deal is made of the need for high-profile athletes to see themselves as role models, and that's no doubt true. But, as I've been emphasizing throughout this book, it's essential for us to think primarily in terms of *ourselves* more than anyone else.

In terms of *my* being a role model and in terms of *my* responsibility as a role model.

Think of it in this straightforward way: If you're old enough to read this book, you're old enough to be thinking seriously about being a role model.

No matter if you are a high school, college, Olympic, or professional athlete, coach, or fan, no matter who you are and what level of sport you're involved with, the influence that you have on others can never—never—be underestimated.

Your influence on those younger than you, close to you, watching you, listening to you, sitting next to you, guarding you, cheering for you, asking you for an autograph, competing against you—on those you would never have dreamed of influencing.

No matter who I am, **I AM A ROLE MODEL.**

That's the starting point when it comes to being a role model: If you're breathing and you're in contact with other people, then you're a role model.

Period.

❝What you are thunders so that I cannot hear what you say to the contrary.❞
Ralph Waldo Emerson

Being a Good Role Model

The fact that we are all role models is important, but it's just a *starting* point. We still haven't gotten to the more important point.

As a hot-under-the-collar high school principal once told a half-dozen of her school's football players who had trouble the night before remembering that they were role models: "That's the way it is, now deal with it—or else!"

Deal with it—or else.

Strong words, yes. But sometimes strong words are needed to help us appreciate a strong reality. Such as taking seriously that we are role models and should deal with it responsibly. In other words, such as our responsibility to be *good* role models.

And that's the more important point: It's up to us not to settle for just being role models, but to do our best to be *good* role models.

You see, accepting that we are role models is one thing, but how we are dealing with it is another issue. And how we deal with it is completely up to each of us. To *me*.

Make no mistake about it, in one way or another we are *always* dealing with it. If we can't avoid being role models—if we can't avoid influencing others—then we certainly can't avoid dealing with it. It's always there, whether we're playing a game in front of a standing-room-only crowd or not. The real issue is always going to be of *how* we're dealing with it, whether we're dealing with it *well* or not.

When you get right down to it, this widely discussed issue of role models ultimately leaves us with one all-important question to ask ourselves at any given moment:

Am I being a good *role model or a* bad *role model?*

That's the question.

The question is never whether I'm going to be a role model—that's a given.

The question is always whether I'm doing my best to be a *good* role model.

If we truly care about how we're influencing others, it's the question that matters most.

It matters most, of course, because answering it honestly will give us a good indication of how we are affecting the attitudes and conduct of those around us: whether we're being a good influence or a bad influence, whether we're setting a good example or a bad example.

It matters most because of a cardinal rule about the seriousness of being a role model, a rule we'd be wise to remember: Values are *caught* much more often than they are *taught,* and many people are constantly *catching* what we dish out—good *and* bad—whether we realize it or not.

OK, we've defined the question that matters most, but asking it is just the beginning. What matters most in answering this question that matters most? In other words, what's going to decide whether you are being a good or bad role model? No surprise here: *What you are and what you are doing with what you are.* We're right back to the bottom-line issue of personal character.

At this point I could give several examples of what being a good role model and being a bad role model both mean, but I'd simply be repeating myself.

Do you see why?

We've been discussing character, sportsmanship, and ethics, doing the right thing—and all of these things are at the heart of what it means to be a good role model. It's just that when we talk in terms of being a "good role model," we're talking about being a good, sportsmanlike, and ethical person *because* of the way our character and actions affect those around us.

Being a good role model means setting a good example by doing the right thing, the sportsmanlike thing, the ethical thing. Just as being a bad role model means setting a bad example by doing the wrong thing, the unsportsmanlike thing, the unethical thing.

And in the long run—with a lot of heart, determination, and practice—we hope to be exceptional role models who do the right thing naturally and consistently. That way, other people can *always* trust our personal character and the actions that flow from it. They can *always* depend on the example we set. They can *always* have faith that our influence will be a positive one.

Just as we always trust, depend on, and have faith in our own truly exceptional role models.

⚜

Here's a quote that nicely summarizes the points I've made about role models. It's from an opinion piece by Utah Jazz basketball star Karl Malone in the June 14, 1993, issue of *Sports Illustrated*. A close friend of Charles Barkley, Malone wrote the article for *SI* shortly after Barkley's "I am not a role model" commercial started airing.

Charles, you can deny being a role model all you want, but I don't think it's your decision to make. We don't choose to be role models, we are chosen. Our only choice is whether to be a good role model or a bad one. . . . I love being a role model, and I try to be a positive one. That doesn't mean I always succeed. I'm no saint. I make mistakes, and sometimes I do childish things. And I don't always wake up in a great, role-model mood. . . . But you don't have to be perfect to be a good role model, and people shouldn't expect perfection. If I were deciding whether a basketball player was a positive role model, I would want to know: Does he influence people's lives in a positive way away from the court? . . . Does he display the values—like honesty and determination—that are part of being a good person?

66 The true athlete should have character, not be a character. 99
John Wooden

Choosing Role Models

Sir Charles's ad-itude may have shot an air ball with its opening "I am not a role model" line, but it made a decisive slam dunk with its statement that "parents should be role models."

Of course, the main point of that statement was that parents, not professional athletes, should assume *primary* responsibility for being role models to their children—which is profoundly true.

But it's also profoundly true from the standpoint of *choosing* role models, and that's what we'll focus on next: Choosing role models—especially choosing high-profile athletes and coaches as role models.

It may seem that a discussion about choosing role models isn't directly related to personal character, but it is.

When we talk about *choosing* role models, we will no doubt be talking about someone else's character. But if we think about it carefully, especially in terms of how someone else's character can really influence our own character, we can begin to see how closely related choices in role models can be to the shaping of our personal character.

Remember the cardinal rule in the last chapter about values being *caught* more than *taught*? It works both ways: from the standpoint of *my* being a role model as well as from the standpoint of *my* being influenced by the people I choose as role models. Other people definitely "catch" our attitudes and behavior, but we also "catch" other people's attitudes and behavior, especially from those people we most admire and look up to—our role models.

(Have you noticed how we use the language of role models? When we talk from the standpoint of *Me* being a role model, we usually emphasize that *I* should be "a *good* role model." But when we talk about our choosing someone else as a role model, we never say he or she is "my *good* role model," because "good" is understood implicitly. We just say he or she is "my role model," and for us that almost always has a positive meaning. I mention this because it might help clear up any confusion.)

The upshot here is that no matter how we interpret the question "Are athletes role models?"—whether in terms of their *being* role models or in terms of *choosing* them as role models—the answer will be connected in one way or another to our own character.

Thus, we could say that

> if it's a question of *being* a role model,
> the answer will follow along these lines:

> *I am a role model,*
> *so I should do my best to be a* good *role model;*

> and if it's a question of *choosing* role models,
> the answer will follow along these lines:

> *Since my role models greatly influence my character,*
> I should do my best to choose, learn from, and imitate
> good *role models.*

The question we're focusing on here, of course, is whether we should choose celebrity athletes and coaches as our role models. Are they good choices for us to learn from and imitate?

It's important to realize that we're not merely talking about learning from and imitating their athletic skills. We're talking about learning from and imitating their personal characters and the actions that flow from their characters. We're talking about choosing people who do the right thing—the ethical and sportsmanlike thing—naturally and consistently.

What do you think? Are there any high-profile athletes or coaches you consider to be among your greatest role models in this sense?

Charles Barkley's attitude seems to be that professional athletes such as himself should *not* be our role models—at least not our primary role models.

There's a lot of wisdom in this part of his ad-itude. In fact, we could even go so far as to say that the world of professional sports usually *doesn't* provide us with the best choices in role models.

No, I'm not going to make any sweeping judgments about the personal character of star athletes and coaches, because that would obviously go against the Golden Rule message I've been emphasizing. Sweeping judgments are sweeping judgments. If they are unfair and uncalled for, then they'll be just as unfair and uncalled for when we're talking about the world of high-profile and high-stakes sports.

The point isn't that there are no genuine role models in high-profile sports or that all celebrity athletes and coaches have bad character. Again, that would be making a sweeping judgment that would be not only unfair but *false*.

Take your pick from the past or present—Arthur Ashe, David Robinson, Mary Lou Retton, Cal Ripken Jr., Grant Hill, Chris Evert, Julius Erving, Tommy Lasorda, Hakeem Olajuwon, Bonnie Blair, John Thompson, Kirby Puckett, Sheryl Swoops, Barry Sanders, Nolan Ryan, Pat Summitt, George Raveling, Joe Dumars, George "Sparky" Anderson, Nancy Lopez, Michael Chang, Fernando Valenzuela, Joe Montana, Jackie Joyner-Kersee, Mike Krzyzewski, Wayne Gretzky, Gail Devers, Gene Stallings—athletes and coaches such as these have consistently given us reason to believe they are models of good character. A couple of them, in fact, continue to be role models of mine. So, obviously, role models can be found in professional athletics.

But—and this is a big "but"—at best, they're usually going to be *secondary* role models for us. That's the crucial point to keep in mind.

There is a lot of wisdom in Barkley's lines about who should and should not be our primary role models, and for one simple reason: When it comes down to this very important business of choosing, learning from, and imitating role models, *the fact of the matter is that very few of us ever really get to* know *high-profile athletes and coaches.*

We can certainly learn from them, but almost always in a limited way.

Because despite all that we read in the sports pages; despite all that we see and hear about sports on TV; and despite all those pages we pore over in sports biographies and autobiographies, we can never really get to know these athletes and coaches. We sometimes like to think we do, but we really don't. What we do know, and know well, is primarily exterior. Game face. Persona, but not necessarily substance.

A character, definitely, but not necessarily *character*.

As much as we may not want to admit it, we would be kidding ourselves if we didn't accept the fact that choosing our role models from the world of pro sports (translation: from the world of professional entertainment) can be risky business.

For the overwhelming majority of us, what we know about celebrity athletes and coaches ends at exactly the point where the media-hyped images and descriptions end. We seldom get to know what kind of people they really are, what their true character is really like. In the most important ways, we just don't *know* them. For all practical purposes, they are *strangers* to us.

All of this is just another way of saying that we need to keep the world of pro sports in perspective. More than anything else, pro sports is a world of entertainment and big business. And sometimes, by its very nature, it's a world of make-believe. None of this means that world is bad; it just means we can't always depend on what we see and hear there.

---

66 It's time for us to start choosing our heroes more carefully, rather than letting others choose them for us. 99

Karen Grigsby Bates

That's why it's important that we look for our primary role models in places that are much more familiar to us. Like home, school, church, recreational parks, doctors' offices, fire stations, police stations, hardware stores, grocery stores—our own neighborhoods.

These places usually provide us with the best and most dependable role models: My mother, unconditional friend. My teacher, cultivator of knowledge and imagination. My doctor, healer of people. My minister, priest, or rabbi, caretaker of enduring truths. My athletic coach, model of fair play and sportsmanship. My neighbor, good Samaritan. My dance instructor, portrayer of grace and discipline. My best friend, keeper of promises and secrets.

What's striking about these examples is that they all come from the low-profile world of what we know—the "real" world. In sharp contrast to our favorite sports celebrities, these people we truly know.

We know their personal character. Not perfectly, but confidently.

They're the people we can depend on when it comes to learning from and imitating good character and the actions that flow from good character.

They are our greatest role models for one simple reason: They have character that we know and can count on.

Ethical Excellence:

The Name of the Game Is Always My Personal Character

It's Never Just a Game

We're now in the homestretch, but we're not going to slow down. We can't afford to coast to the finish; too much is at stake.

Really. The issues we've been looking at are too serious and too far-reaching to take lightly.

In fact, if one message should now be loud and clear, it's this: When looking at sports competition from the standpoint of being good and doing right—from the standpoint of character—*it's never just a game.* And that's true no matter who you are and what kind of competition you're involved in.

Some of the most powerful words I have ever read about the serious ethical dimension of sports come from a speech given by legendary track and field coach Brutus Hamilton. Olympic athlete, Olympic coach, international ambassador of goodwill, and one of the best track and field coaches ever, Hamilton was by all accounts also notable for his excellence of character.

Coach Hamilton's words in this speech caught many in his audience off guard, since it was made at a sports injury conference and his listeners were expecting him to talk about *physical* injuries. He didn't. There was another class of injuries he considered much more serious, and that's what he was obviously set on discussing.

I consider it a privilege, even a responsibility, to share these timeless words of wisdom with you now:

> We are living in a victory-mad, record-conscious time. There is a professional intensity creeping into interscholastic and intercollegiate sports comparable to the training of the professional ballet dancer. Some of this is good; some of it bad when it interferes with the more serious purposes of life; when it threatens to sow the seeds of moral decay into the lives of our young men and even

into the lives of some of our institutions of higher education. Alumni and even administrators of some of our colleges want victory and some of them are not too particular how the material to assure those victories is brought into the institution, or what becomes of the young men after their competition is completed. "Yes, Victory is great but sometimes when it cannot be helped, Defeat also is great," sang Walt Whitman. No victory is great when it is bought at the sacrifice of ideals: and no defeat is disgraceful as long as one does his best and follows the gleam of idealism. . . .

There is no need here to expand upon the potential values of sport as an adjunct to the educational processes. I shall say only that all of these values lose significance if they are not accompanied by ideals. When ideals are obscured in amateur sports, then comes the danger of an athletic injury to the character of the athlete.

A boy begins to show promise his sophomore year in high school. He gets into a few games or meets. He sees his name in the paper, maybe even his picture. He improves his junior year, is a regular on the team, and his scrapbook gets thick. His senior year he really blossoms out, makes all-state, sets new records, gets notices in all the papers and magazines. He's the most popular man in his student body; every child in the community knows him and tries to emulate him. His parents are proud of him and justly so. He's a good lad.

Colleges begin to rush him in his junior year. They go all out in his senior year. He is invited to visit many campuses, some of them out of state. He accepts as many invitations as time permits. He is shown a wonderful time. He meets the college coaches, talks to some of the athletes on each campus, is shown the athletic facilities, sees some shows, meets some coeds and goes to a dance. He is a little bewildered by it all, but it's good fun and he has a wonderful time on each campus.

Coaches, alumni, and friends of each college drop by his hometown and talk to his folks. They are very skilled in their presentations. They are all good salesmen. This school offers a free ride: board, room, tuition, and some spending money. Another offers tuition and an easy job. Each school offers some kind of financial inducement under one guise or another. The parents listen and become more confused as the summer progresses. They finally leave it up to the boy, and he accepts the offer which seems best suited to his particular inclinations.

It's easy to see where a boy can suffer an athletic injury to his character in such a situation. From his junior year in high school he has been subjected to pressures and publicity. He has been led to believe that he can get something for nothing; that life is going to be all primroses merely because he can run or jump or throw or shoot baskets or evade tacklers. He must have good stuff inside to keep his wits about him. He is called upon at eighteen to make decisions which would challenge those much older and wiser. It is to the everlasting credit of our athletic youth that so many of them turn out well in spite of the temptations put in their way.

Further athletic injuries to the boy's character can result in college. If he has chosen a school where sports are emphasized out of proportion to their importance, he will find life easy if he performs well on the team. He will be coddled, made over, given parties by avid alumni, and even handed under-the-table payment, if not in cash then in some kind of presents. He's embarrassed at first, but soon comes to accept these things as a matter of course. The moral fiber gradually weakens and by the time his intercollegiate competition is over he is a victim of the system, a slave to gross and violent tastes, standing at the crossroads of Destiny. He was yesterday's headlines; he will be tomorrow's trivia. Now comes the harsh test as he faces the cruel pace of this competitive world in what he considers routine, humdrum chores of business. He gets no headlines now; others who are younger are taking his place. Some former athletes make the adjustment rather quickly, others grope for several years and then make the adjustment. . . . Others, all too many, drift into middle age and resort to artificial stimulation to substitute for the intoxicating experiences they enjoyed in sports. Maybe sports were only partly to blame, but I believe no one would criticize a doctor who diagnosed these cases as an "athletic injury to character suffered in youth."

The athletic injury to the mind is perhaps a little more tangible. First, there is the bright lad in the high school who has a high IQ and is capable of making grades sufficiently high to qualify for admission to any college. But he gets carried away by the publicity and hero worship he receives in high school due to his athletic attainments. His grades slump, he ignores the admonitions of his coach and counselors and is content to merely pass. He gets his diploma but is disgusted with himself to find that he can't qualify for any first-rate college. He goes through a bad period of depression.

We have a number of these boys at the University of California. They are the ones who woke up. Many of them went into the Army or worked for a couple of years after high school. Then they went to junior college and made up their grades. They do superior work at the university, but they don't go out for sports. They've had enough. A doctor might diagnose their case as "suffered an athletic injury to the mind in high school—fully recovered."

The sad cases, though, are the ones which involve the eager, bright lad who goes to college on some kind of an athletic grant and is eager to become an engineer, lawyer, doctor, teacher, or architect.

He becomes a victim of the intensity of the athletic training program. He misses practice to work on problem sets or to write out a book report. The coach suggests that he may be in the wrong course. Maybe he should transfer to a course which is not so demanding on his time. He certainly can't miss any more practices or his grant may be terminated. The boy has little choice, so he submits to the coach' s suggestion and gives up his planned career. He may succeed gloriously in this new field, but always he will wonder if he didn't make a mistake. He will always consider that he suffered an athletic injury to his mind in college whether anyone else does or not. When the training for an intercollegiate team becomes so time consuming, so intense, and so exhausting that it is no longer possible for the student in the sciences or professions to participate, then something is wrong. Someone, perhaps a great many, are suffering an athletic injury to the mind.

Powerful and timely words—words that Hamilton spoke in 1962. Words that not only speak for themselves but also summarize most of the important points I've emphasized thus far:

- "[W]hen [professional intensity] threatens to sow the seeds of moral decay into the lives of our young men and even into the lives of some of our institutions of higher education."—(The destructive effects of "no place for second place" attitudes.)
- "No victory is great when it is bought at the sacrifice of ideals: and no defeat is disgraceful as long as one does his best and follows the gleam of idealism. . . ."—(Good character is needed to do the right thing, to follow the ideals of sportsmanship, to keep things in perspective.)
- *"When ideals are obscured in amateur sports, then comes the danger of an athletic injury to the character of the athlete."*—(Sportsmanship and ethics go hand in hand. When it comes to ideals and character, it's never just a game, it's serious business.)
- *"He's the most popular man in his student body; every child in the community knows him and tries to emulate him."*—(Athletes are role models, and their being good role models is important.)

- *"He must have good stuff inside to keep his wits about him."*—(We must have excellence in personal character.)
- *"It is to the everlasting credit of our athletic youth that so many of them turn out well in spite of the temptations put in their way."*—(We need to see the good as well as the bad. Do not give up hope. Things are not always as bad as they might seem.)

" Yes, Victory is great but sometimes when it cannot be helped, Defeat is also great."

Walt Whitman

A Gold Medal Perspective

Having a balanced perspective about winning and having the character to maintain that balanced perspective—this enduring message was at the heart of Coach Hamilton's 1962 speech about the serious, "it's never just a game" side of sports competition.

And that's the timeless message with which we're going to bring our discussion about ethical excellence in sports full circle.

Of the many important points I've tried to drive home—about the realities and dangers of unsportsmanlike pollution, about taking sportsmanship and ethics seriously, about being and choosing good role models, and especially about how all these things depend on *my* personal character—I still haven't emphasized enough how *my* personal perspective on winning relates to *my* personal character.

The connection has been there all along, especially when we were focusing on the "no place for second place" attitude, but it hasn't quite been nailed down.

It's important to nail it down, because our personal perspective on winning is at the heart of our personal quest for ethical excellence—which, of course, is just another way of saying that it's at the very heart of our personal character.

Our personal perspective on winning is at the very heart of our personal character.

This point may not hit home immediately. It may be one of those points you have to think about for a while until it sinks in: *My* personal perspective on winning is at the heart of *my* personal character. And keep in mind that "for a while until it sinks in" doesn't necessarily mean for a few hours, a few days, or even a few years. In fact, as many world-class athletes and coaches have admitted, sometimes it can take *a long time* and *a lot of competitive experience* for it to completely sink in.

One world-class athlete talked to me about the connection between perspective and character as he recalled a momentous day of the 1992 summer Olympic Games in Barcelona, Spain.

I'm most happy to tell you about this world-class athlete, because he also happens to be a role model with world-class personal character.

And he also happens to be a world-class friend of mine.

Until his retirement from competition shortly after the 1992 Games, Terry Schroeder had been one of the top water polo players in the world for more than twelve years. That's twelve years of international competition in one of the world's most physically demanding sports—an amazing athletic accomplishment by any standard.

Terry is a four-time Olympian, selected for the U.S. water polo team in 1980, 1984, 1988, and 1992. (Of course, like all other U.S. Olympic athletes in 1980, he was prevented from competing in the Moscow Games because of the U.S. boycott.) Along with his Olympic water polo teammates, Terry brought home silver medals from both the '84 and '88 Games.

But no medal was brought home from the '92 Barcelona Games.

"Barcelona, by far, was the most disappointing," Terry told me not too long after returning from Spain. "I mean, it was disappointing enough in '84 and '88 to fall just short of winning the gold, but to not take any medal home in '92—as good as we were—that was really hard to swallow."

After a long, reflective pause, he continued:

"But the truth is, in the most important ways Barcelona turned out to be the most rewarding Olympics for me—medal or no medal."

"Why's that?" I asked.

"Basically, it's because of what happened on the way back to the Olympic village after the loss to Spain in the semifinals."

Another reflective pause.

"What happened?" I asked impatiently.

> **❝When the one Great Scorer comes to mark against your name, He writes not that you won or lost but how you played the Game.❞**
>
> **Grantland Rice**

"Lori [his wife] and I were walking back to the village right after the big loss to Spain," he said. "I was feeling really disappointed, angry, and frustrated—all those emotions at once. I was blowing off steam left and right as we walked."

With an intense look and a tone that told me he was reliving the moment, Terry said:

"I kept telling Lori and myself over and over again about the bad calls the refs made, about how we didn't play as well as we should have, and about how we could have won if only the refs hadn't made those bad calls, and if only we had executed this and that play a little better. I kept saying how the loss to Spain meant we were out of gold medal contention, and how *that* meant I was *never* going to win a gold medal because Barcelona would definitely be my last Olympics."

He paused just long enough to sigh.

"Then all of a sudden I cut myself off in mid-sentence, just as my eyes caught a glimpse of Kirk Kilgour coming toward us."

A former Olympian himself, Kirk Kilgour had been one of the top volleyball players in the world during the 1970s. When he was playing professionally in Italy, Kilgour's stellar athletic career was tragically cut short by a freak accident during a team practice session. The accident left him paralyzed from the neck down and confined to a wheelchair.

"Kirk made his way up to us, driving his wheelchair with his tongue—with just his *tongue*," Terry recalled. "Then, with a nice, big smile on his face, he asked us how the game had gone against Spain. I didn't say much of anything. In fact, I didn't hear much of anything that either Lori or Kirk said. I just stood there looking at Kirk in his wheelchair. It was a defining moment for me."

"What do you mean, Terry?" I asked.

"Bumping into Kirk changed my whole perspective on winning and losing. Because, just like that," Terry said, snapping his fingers, "the whole truth of what was going on inside me suddenly hit me like a ton of bricks. Here I was, whining, moaning, and groaning, feeling totally sorry for myself because I hadn't won a gold medal. And there was Kirk, forever confined to a wheelchair, smiling and happy, being very positive about life. What an inspiration!"

With his face growing brighter by the second, Terry continued:

"It became clear to me, then and there, how you can focus so much on winning that it can really affect your character—not to mention the character of those around you. Look, I had absolutely no good reason to complain or feel sorry for myself. I had my health, a supportive family, a successful career as a chiropractor, great friends, and, most of all, Lori. I hate to admit it, but I think at times I let my desire to win a gold medal overshadow the most important things in my life. Standing there in front of Kirk and next to Lori, I finally realized—I mean *really* realized—what it's all about.

"It's not ultimately about medals or win-loss records or getting your picture in the sports pages," Terry added. "Winning is important, but it's not *most* important. What's most important are the internal things—personal growth, improving your character, even developing long-lasting friendships. That's it, the internal things. It's like what John Wooden always emphasized to his players at UCLA: What's most important is what you take away from the game and are able to use for the rest of your life.

"It really is all about what the Olympic creed has always said it's all about:

> *'The important thing in the Olympic Games*
> *is not to win but to take part.*
> *The important thing in life*
> *is not the triumph but the struggle.*
> *The essential thing*
> *is not to have conquered but to have fought well.'*

"That's what it's all about."

A gold medal perspective from one with gold medal character.

Playing to Win

Words to play by. Words to live by.

Hamilton's and Schroeder's hard-hitting words of wisdom echo what all great role-model coaches and athletes try their best to play by and to live by: a balanced perspective. The world-class athletic successes enjoyed by both Hamilton and Schroeder are proof positive that having a balanced perspective on winning does not at all mean playing to lose.

A balanced perspective means:

Sports are important, but not *most* important.
Winning is important, but not *most* important.
The question isn't "Should I play to win?"
but "*How* should I play to win?"
Playing to win is noble,
but not at the sacrifice of sportsmanship and ethics—
not at the sacrifice of *my personal character.*
No one plays to lose,
but losing does not make one a loser.
Everyone plays to win,
but winning does not make one a winner.
First place is great,
but only if there's an honorable place for second place.
Being MVP is great,
but never at the expense of being a good role model.
External rewards can be great,

but never at the expense of internal rewards.
Winning isn't everything, but it is *something.*
Winning isn't the only thing, but it is *something.*
Sports are neither everything nor the only thing, but they
are *something.*
And they are something that can be very good—
if we have the character to keep winning in perspective.

The bottom line is always a matter of *having the character to do what needs to be done.*

Having the character to do what needs to be done means continually and honestly asking ourselves some important questions:

How important is winning to me?
Is it everything to me?
Is it the only thing to me?
How do I define "winning"?
Do I have a balanced perspective on winning?
Does my perspective make a place for second place?

As important as those questions are, they're still a little too abstract. In that form, they're a little too easy for us to manipulate and rationalize in order to make ourselves feel comfortable. Remember: If we sincerely care about what's going on in our sports, good *and* bad, then we'll do our best to find *reality,* not comfort. And finding reality will mean continually and honestly asking ourselves some practical, soul-searching, and gut-checking

---

❝Winning isn't everything, but making the effort to win is.❞

Vince Lombardi

questions—questions that can powerfully reveal the connection between our personal perspective on winning and our personal character:

How far am I willing to go in order to win?
What am I willing to sacrifice to win—besides my time
and energy?
Am I willing to sacrifice
my health?
My friendships?
My family?
My team's reputation?
My school's reputation?
My community's reputation?
My reputation?
My principles?
My integrity?
Exactly where will I draw the line—if anywhere—
when it comes to winning?

Playing by the Rules

It is an undeniable fact of human life that *lines must be drawn and respected.*

If we don't draw lines, or if we pretend there aren't any lines to be drawn, we self-destruct. End of story.

Call it "the bottom line on lines": *There are always lines that need to be drawn and respected for our own good.*

This holds true no matter which part of our lives we're talking about: health, relationships, academics, work, finances, whatever.

And it holds true for sportsmanship and sports—any type, any level. It's not as though we automatically have the right to ignore and disrespect lines just because we're talking about *games.*

Again, when it comes to sportsmanship, ethics, and fair play, it's never *just* a game. It's always serious business.

Having the character to respect and abide by lines—in other words, by *rules*—is one of the most important points concerning sportsmanship, ethics, and fair play.

But there are three related points that still have to be made. And all three points can help nail down why the name of the game is always *my personal character.*

First, *playing by the rules and keeping winning in perspective go hand in hand.*

If we're doing one, we're likely to be doing the other. If we're not doing one, we're not likely to be doing the other.

66 You can follow all the rules and still be unethical. 99

R. G.

Unsportsmanlike pollution—like the "no place for second place" attitude—can be generated either by cheating or by an unbalanced perspective on winning, but when these two things are so closely tied that they're actually feeding each other, there's the potential for some clouds of dangerously bad air.

On the other hand, of course, if a respect for the rules and a balanced perspective are feeding each other, there's the potential for some refreshing, character-building blasts of clean air.

The name of the game? *My personal character:*

> If I have the character to keep winning in perspective,
> I'll have the character to play by the rules.
> If I don't, I won't.

> If I have the character to play by the rules,
> I'll have the character to keep things in perspective.
> If I don't, I won't.

Second, *playing by the rules is playing the game; not playing by the rules is not playing the game.*

We can try all we want to get around this point, but its logic and truth are inescapable.

How can we say we have really "won"—not to mention how can we feel good about ourselves—if we have cheated? Think about it: A game is defined by its rules, and if we're not playing by its rules, then we're not playing the game. And there's no way to truly "win" it if we're not. Cheaters are never winners.

Yes, it's possible that no one else will know we've cheated, and that we can go on acting as if we did win, but deep down there is no way to deny that we never really won in the first place. We lose the moment we cheat. We make ourselves losers the moment we cheat.

No one else may ever know that we cheated, but that doesn't change the truth of the situation one bit.

The name of the game? *My personal character:*

> If I have the character to play by the rules, then I have the character to play the game.
> *Which means I have the character to win.*

> If I don't have the character to play by the rules, then I don't have the character to play the game.
> *Which means I don't have the character to win.*

Third, and this is the clincher, *being sportsmanlike and being a good role model mean much more than just playing by the rules.*

This is one of the most crucial points that needs to be driven home. Being sportsmanlike, being ethical, being fair, being a good role model—in short, *doing the right thing*—is never a matter of just following a rule book. It's much more. And this "much more" is going to fall squarely on your personal character.

Why? Because rule books can't possibly cover all situations. There are many times when a rule book will not be able to tell you the right thing to do. And even if a rule book gives you a general principle to follow, it may still be up to you, to your personal character, to determine specifically the right thing to do.

But there's another way of emphasizing this point, a way that is perhaps as effective and strong as any: *You can follow all the rules and still be unsportsmanlike or unethical.*

That may not be obvious at first glance. What it ultimately means is that just because you play by the rules does not *by itself* mean that you play fairly. Or that you are sportsmanlike. Or that you are a good role model.

There are a lot of things you may be doing that may not be covered by the written rules but that everyone knows are wrong, such as lying, taking advantage of someone, cutting someone down, being prejudiced because of someone's ethnicity or gender or religion, being greedy, being selfish, and on and on.

The name of the game? *My personal character:*

While I must have the character to play by the rules,
I must also have the character
to do the right thing when the rules don't help.

If I want to have the character to be a good role model,
then I must have the character
to go above and beyond the rules.

If I want to have the character
to strive for ethical excellence,
then I must have the character
to draw the line when there is no line drawn.

Playing for Keeps

Sow an act and you reap a habit.
Sow a habit and you reap a character.
Sow a character and you reap a destiny.
—Charles Reade

There it is, in three easy to remember lines.

There, in one short quote—one of my all-time favorites—we have the core message of our discussion.

There, in four key words, we have the basic formula for ethical excellence:

Act ➜ Habit ➜ Character ➜ Destiny

I strongly encourage you to write down this quote or formula on a sheet of paper and put it where you can see it often, whether in your locker, your locker room, your gym, your car, your bedroom, your office, wherever.

Since it's the formula for any kind of excellence, it can be a reminder of what it takes to achieve athletic excellence. Or academic excellence. Or artistic excellence.

Over and above these, it can be a reminder of what it ultimately takes to achieve the most important excellence of all: ethical excellence.

And it can be a reminder of the single greatest reason why ethical excellence in sports is serious business, never just a game: because it's about *my personal destiny.*

It's not only about the future of sports. Nor is it only about the future of our society. While it's about sports and—much more importantly—about our society, it's also very much about the future of *me*:

My acts ➔ My habits ➔ My character ➔ My destiny

This brings up two extremely important final points:

*When it comes to achieving
or not achieving ethical excellence,
I, and I alone, ultimately determine my destiny.*

And:

*Even when I am playing sports,
I am in the process of determining my destiny.*

That's why we shouldn't play simply to win, but should play while keeping perspective.

That's why we should play for the long haul, and why we should play using and seeking excellence of character.

And that's why *the road to ethical excellence in sports runs through my personal character.*

The ball is ultimately in *my* court.

It will never be in anyone else's court.

---

66 **Destiny is no matter of chance. It is a matter of choice: It is not a thing to be waited for, it is a thing to be achieved.** **99**

William Jennings Bryan

Extra Points: Taking It to the Next Level

A Three-Point Sportsmanship Checklist

1. *Is it against the rules?*
2. *Is it fair to everyone involved?*
3. *Would my ethical role models do it?*

Unfortunately, it's a fact of life that we will be faced occasionally with difficult ethical situations in which we don't know the right thing to do.

Fortunately, these difficult situations—or ethical dilemmas—are the exception rather than the rule in our lives.

But even if they don't happen that often, they *do* happen. And when they do, they're far from fun. In fact, ethical dilemmas can present us with some of the most gut-wrenching and mind-boggling decisions that we will ever have to make.

I'm offering this three-point sportsmanship checklist as a tool that can help you resolve ethical dilemmas—in or out of sports. Keep in mind, however, that there is no absolutely fail-safe method for resolving ethical dilemmas. They're not like algebra problems, where we can always count on some formula to give us the right answer.

Nonetheless, even if the checklist itself doesn't immediately give you the right answer, most of the time it can point you in the right direction—and that's half the battle when it comes to ethical dilemmas.

Finally, I would suggest two rules of thumb for using the checklist. First, ask the three questions in the order they are given. This may not always be necessary, but it's logical, especially if you begin with concrete written rules—if it's against the rules, there's probably no reason to continue down the list.

Second—and more important—if you answer "no" to *any* of the three questions, then most likely, you have the answer you're looking for.

Of course, if you know *that,* then it becomes a matter of your having the character to do the right thing.

Ask yourself:

1. *Is it against the rules?*
   - The rules of the game?
   - Of my league or conference?
   - Of my association or federation?
   - Of my school?
   - Of law?

2. *Is it fair to everyone involved?*
   - To my opponents?
   - To my team?
   - To game officials?
   - To fans?
   - To my school?
   - To myself?

3. *Would my ethical role models do it?*
   - Who are my ethical role models?
   - How would they feel about me if I did it?
   - How would I feel about them if they did it?
   - Do I have time to get their advice first?
   - Do I have the courage to do what they would do?

Resources:
Books

All of the books listed here have two things in common: I am in their debt, and I highly recommend them.

All of them have directly or indirectly helped shape the writing of this book, and all of them can take you much farther and higher with the themes in *Character Is Everything*.

Books that discuss ethical issues in sports from a philosophical point of view (whether throughout or in useful chapters and sections):

Fair Play: Sports, Values, and Society. Robert L. Simon. Westview Press, Boulder, CO, 1991. ISBN 0-8133-7974-1.

Philosophic Inquiry in Sport. William Morgan and Klaus Meier, eds. Human Kinetics Publishers, Champaign-Urbana, IL, 1988. ISBN 0-87322-119-2.

Philosophy of Sport. Drew Hyland. Paragon House, New York, NY, 1990. ISBN 1-55778-189-3.

Practical Philosophy of Sport. Scott Kretchmar. Human Kinetics Publishers, Champaign-Urbana, IL, 1994. ISBN: 0-87322-619-4.

Books that discuss from a coach's point of view the importance of having character and building character:

Beyond Winning: The Timeless Wisdom of Great Philosopher Coaches. Gary M. Walton. Leisure Press, Champaign, IL, 1992. ISBN 0-88011-453-3.

Positive Coaching: Building Character and Self-Esteem Through Sports. Jim Thompson. Warde Publishers, Portola Valley, CA, 1995. ISBN 1-886346-00-3.

The Winner Within: A Life Plan for Team Players. Pat Riley. G.P. Putnam's Sons, New York, NY, 1993. ISBN 0-399-13839-0.

Books that discuss ethics (in general) from the standpoint of character education:

Educating for Character. Thomas Lickona. Bantam Books, New York, NY, 1991. ISBN 0-553-37052-9.

Reclaiming Our Schools: A Handbook on Teaching Character, Academics, and Discipline. Edward Wynne and Kevin Ryan. Merrill Publishing, New York, NY, 1993. ISBN 0-02-430755-0.

Why Johnny Can't Tell Right from Wrong. William Kilpatrick. Simon and Schuster, New York, NY, 1992. ISBN 0-671-75801-2.

Books that provide introductory discussions of ethical theory:

A Handbook for Ethics. Robert C. Solomon. Harcourt Brace College Publishers, Fort Worth, TX, 1996. ISBN 0-15-502964-9.

Vice and Virtue in Everyday Life: Introductory Readings in Ethics. Christina Sommers and Fred Sommers. Harcourt Brace Jovanovich College Publishers, Fort Worth, TX, 1993. ISBN 0-15-500375.

A book that defends, with compelling evidence, the educational and social value of school sports:

The Importance of School Sports in American Education and Socialization. Ronald M. Jeziorski. University Press of America, Lanham, MD, 1994. ISBN 0-8191-9489-1.

A book that can satisfy most sports ethics bibliographical needs (at least for works published before 1991):

Sports Ethics in America: A Bibliography 1970–1990. Donald Jones. Greenwood Press, Westport, CT, 1992. ISBN 0-313-27767-2.

Resources:
Organizations

Below are listed some organizations that, in one way or another, are involved in promoting issues of sportsmanship, sports ethics, or character education in sports. Most of these organizations can provide helpful resource materials of one kind or another—including in written, audio, or video form.

Amateur Athletic Foundation
(AAF)
2141 West Adams Blvd.
Los Angeles, CA 90018-2040
(213) 730-9600
fax: (213) 730-9637

Amateur Athletic Union (AAU)
3400 West 86th St.
PO Box 68207
Indianapolis, IN 46268
(317) 872-2900
fax: (317) 875-0548

American Baseball Coaches
Association (ABCA)
108 South University Ave.
Suite 3
Mount Pleasant, MI 48858-2327
(517) 775-3300
fax: (517) 775-3600

American Football Coaches
Association (AFCA)
5900 Old McGregor Rd.

Waco, TX 76712
(817) 776-5900
fax: (817) 776-3744

American Legion Baseball
(ALB)
PO Box 1055
Indianapolis, IN 46206
(317) 630-1213
fax: (317) 630-1280

American Sports Education
Institute (ASEI)
200 Castlewood Drive
North Palm Beach, FL 33408
(407) 842-4100
fax: (407) 863-8984

American Sports Education
Program (ASEP)
PO Box 5076
Champaign, IL 61825-5076
(800) 747-5698
fax: (217) 351-2674

American Youth Soccer
Organization
(AYSO)
PO Box 5045
Hawthorne, CA 90251-5045
(800) USA-AYSO
fax: (213) 643-5310

Black Coaches Association
(BCA)
PO Box J
Des Moines, IA 50311
(515) 271-3010

Center for the Study of Sport
Northeastern University
360 Huntington Ave., 161 CP
Boston, MA 02115
(617) 437-4025
fax: (617) 373-4566

College Football Association
(CFA)
6688 Gunpark Drive
Suite 201
Boulder, CO 80301
(303) 530-5566
fax: (303) 530-5371

The Communitarian Network
2130 H St. NW
Suite 714J
Washington, DC 20052
(202) 994-7997
fax: (202) 994-1606

Fellowship of Christian Athletes
(FCA)
8701 Leeds Rd.
Kansas City, MO 64129
(816) 921-0909
fax: (816) 921-8755

Institute for International Sport
306 Adams Hall

The University of Rhode Island
Kingston, RI 02881
(401) 792-2375
fax: (401) 792-2429

Knight Foundation Commission
on Intercollegiate Athletics
John S. and James L. Knight
Foundation
One Biscayne Tower,
Suite 3800
2 South Biscayne Blvd.
Miami, FL 33131-1803
(305) 539-0009

Little League Baseball (LLB)
PO Box 3485
Williamsport, PA 17701
(717) 326-1921
fax: (717) 326-1074

National Association for Sport
and Physical Education
(NASPE)
1900 Association Drive
Reston, VA 22091
(703) 476-3410
fax: (703) 476-8316

National Association of
Basketball Coaches
(NABC)
9300 West 110th St.
Suite 640
Overland Park, KS 66210
(913) 469-1001
fax: (913) 469-1390

National Association of
Collegiate Athletic Directors
(NACAD)
PO Box 16428
Cleveland, OH 44116
(216) 892-4000
fax: (216) 892-4007

National Association of
Intercollegiate Athletics (NAIA)
6120 South Yale Ave., Suite 1450
Tulsa, OK 74136-4223
(918) 494-8828

National Association of Sports
Officials (NASO)
2017 Lathrop Ave.
Racine, WI 53405
(414) 632-5448
fax: (414) 632-5460

National Collegiate Athletic
Association (NCAA)
6201 College Blvd.
Overland Park, KS 66211-2422
(913) 339-1906

National Federation
Interscholastic Coaches
Association (NFICA)
11724 Northwest Plaza Circle
PO Box 20626
Kansas City, MO 64195-0626
(816) 464-5400

National Federation
Interscholastic Officials
Association (NFIOA)
11724 Northwest Plaza Circle
PO Box 20626
Kansas City, MO 64195-0626
(816) 464-5400

National Federation of State
High School Associations
(NFSHSA)
11724 Norhwest Plaza Circle
PO Box 20626
Kansas City, MO 64195-0626
(816) 464-5400
fax: (816) 464-5571

National High School Athletic
Coaches Association
(NHSACA)
PO Box 5020
Winter Park, FL 32793
(407) 679-1414

National Intramural-Recreational
Sports Association (NIRSA)
850 Southwest 15th St.
Corvallis, OR 97333
(503) 737-2088
fax: (503) 737-2026

National Junior College Athletic
Association (NJCAA)
PO Box 7305
Colorado Springs, CO 80933-7305
(719) 590-9788
fax: (719) 590-7324

National Soccer Coaches
Association of America (NSCAA)
4220 Shawnee Mission Parkway
Suite 105-B
Fairway, KS 66205
(913) 362-1747
fax: (913) 362-3439

National Youth Sports Coaches
Association (NYSCA)
2611 Old Okeechobee Rd.
West Palm Beach, FL 33409
(800) 729-2057
(407) 684-1141
fax: (407) 684-2546

People-to-People Sports
Committee (PTPSC)
80 Cutter Mill Rd.
Suite 208
Great Neck, NY 11021
(516) 482-5158
fax: (516) 482-3239

Pop Warner Football (PWF)
920 Town Center Drive
Suite I-25
Longhorne, PA 10047
(215) 752-2691
fax: (215) 752-2879

Special Olympics International
(SOI)
1325 G St.
Suite 500
Washington, DC 20005
(202) 628-3630
fax: (202) 824-0200

United States Athletes
Association (USAA)
3735 Lakeland Avenue N, Suite
230
Minneapolis, MN 55422
(612) 522-5844

United States Olympic
Committee (USOC)
Olympic Plaza
Colorado Springs, CO 80909-
5760
(719) 632-5551
fax: (719) 578-4677

United States Organization for
Disabled Athletes (USODA)
c/o John Hurley
143 California Ave.
Uniondale, NY 11553-1131
(516) 485-3701
fax: (516) 485-3707

United States Tennis Association
(USTA)
1212 Avenue of the Americas
New York, NY 10036
(914) 696-7000
fax: (914) 696-7167

U.S. Sports Academy
1 Academy Drive
Daphne, AL 36526
(334) 626-3303
fax: (334) 626-3874

U.S. Youth Soccer Association
(USYSA)
899 Presidential Drive
Suite 117
Richardson, TX 75081
(214) 235-4499
fax: (214) 235-4480

Women's Basketball Coaches
Association (WBCA)
4646 B Lawrenceville Highway
Lilburn, GA 30247
(404) 279-8027
fax: (404) 279-8473

Womens Sports Foundation
Eisenhower Park
East Meadow, NY 11554
(800) 227-3988
fax: (516) 542-4716

The author welcomes your feedback and questions.
You may write to him at:

Dr. Russell W. Gough
Pepperdine University
Humanities Division
Malibu, CA 90263

Dr. Gough can also be contacted via e-mail at:

rgough@pepperdine.edu